WRITING THE PAST IMPERFECT

D. C. Zook

SHANTIWALA
BOOKS
Berkeley, CA

Aside from brief quotations for media coverage and reviews, no part of this book may be reproduced or distributed in any form without the author's permission.

Text copyright © 2018 by D. C. Zook
All rights reserved.
Published by Shantiwala Books (Berkeley, CA)
Cover design by James, GoOnWrite.com
ISBN: 1947609106
ISBN-13 (print): 9781947609105
ISBN-13 (E-book): 9781947609020

Ourselves Among Others:
The Extravagant Failure of Diversity in America
and An Epic Plan to Make It Work

Understanding the Misunderstanding (vol. 1)

Liberating the Enclave (Vol. 2)

Writing the Past Imperfect (vol. 3)

Unpoisoning the Well (vol. 4)

To the spirit and memory of Maruyama Masao, whose work taught me that rewriting history could rewrite the world anew

TABLE OF CONTENTS

Preface to Part 3	Writing the Past Imperfect	ix
Chapter 1	History is a Nice Story	1
Chapter 2	Educating Diversity	57
Chapter 3	We are all Imperialists Now	108
Index		171
About the Author		175

PREFACE TO PART 3

WRITING THE PAST IMPERFECT

Too many people think of history as little more than a chronological list of names and dates. Part of the reason for this is that far too many people suffered through poorly-taught history classes which consisted in fact of little more than the monotonous memorization of a chronological list of names and dates. History, however, is far more than that. History is an extraordinarily powerful force in the crafting of human identity, and Part 3 of this series is dedicated to unmasking the many ways that history is used, misused, and abused in the service of diversity and the ways that the persistent distortion of history has contributed to the extravagant failure of diversity that is the focus of this series.

Chapter 1 shows how history has taken on a central role in debates about diversity, where it is used to bolster claims of group-based solidarity, or to document a history of group-based discrimination and victimization. The result has been a continuous revision of the history of America, but one that has created only more divisiveness rather than greater understanding. This chapter focuses specifically on the question of whether "advocacy histories" help or hinder the process of mutual understanding (arguing that they in fact hinder the process more than help).

Chapter 2 explains why "diversity education" as it is currently taught in our schools fails to teach or cultivate any sort of meaningful diversity. Instead of offering a curriculum that teaches different identity groups to understand one another, diversity education acts as a forum for cultural solidarity, encouraging students to focus on their own identity rather than on the identities of others. This chapter argues for a transformation of the entire diversity curriculum in America, starting with history, with a focus on multicultural education in universities and K-12 programs.

Chapter 3 shows why getting diversity wrong can have tragic and deadly consequences. The Islamic State (IS, or ISIS, or ISIL), for instance, has engaged in an ongoing campaign of extreme brutality and terrorist violence, fueled in part by the mistaken belief that European imperialism "stole" the rightful place of Islam in history and that the Islamic State can somehow reset the clock and put history back on the "right" track (by restoring the Caliphate, among other things). Many other less-extreme groups share this point of view, that history somehow "went wrong" at one specific moment in time, namely, with the rise of European imperialism. This chapter shows how imperialism has been a constant part of human history, long before the European variety emerged, and also shows how efforts to use diversity to set history right can only end in failure and division.

CHAPTER 1

HISTORY IS A NICE STORY

In the classic film *Eyes Without a Face* (*Les yeux sans visage*, 1960), directed by Georges Franju, a doctor becomes obsessed with the idea of restoring his daughter's face after she is badly disfigured in an automobile accident. The doctor, along with his female laboratory assistant, connive together to lure young and beautiful girls into the doctor's lab where they remove their faces and attempt to graft them onto the face of the doctor's daughter. While the daughter suffers and endures the horrifying plans of her father, she is forced to wear a mask over her face—a featureless mask that covers everything except her eyes. The doctor is obsessed with restoring the surface beauty of his daughter, even to the point of murdering other women to steal their faces. For him, the cost is irrelevant when the end result is unblemished beauty. The daughter, however, comes to accept her disfigured condition over time, learning the lesson that physical beauty is only one superficial aspect of her identity and despairing of the ugly violence wrought by her father in the endless effort to restore her lost beauty. She eventually resolves to escape from her father's experiments and to accept her condition, blemishes and all, as her true identity. In the final scene, her father is attacked by his own guard dogs, who cleverly deploy canine irony and badly maul and disfigure the doctor's own face during the attack.

I reference this film because the plot is reminiscent of one of the more troubling aspects of diversity. Operating under the assumption that outsiders—through the "accident" of decades or even centuries of oppression—have in essence disfigured their history, identity-based groups have been busy in the laboratory of diversity trying to rewrite their history in a way that removes the alleged disfigurement and leaves behind only the unblemished historical beauty that they believe would and should have been there all along, if not for this unfortunate accident of history. In every part where outsiders have attributed any sort of negative characteristic—backward, primitive, barbaric, violent, and so on—the historical surgeons excise the disfigurement and substitute a new image supplied by insiders that reverses the disfigurement and leaves behind a beautiful historical visage. There are even those who believe that this mission is so central to the project of diversity that outsiders should not even be allowed to write the history of other groups at all.[1] Only insiders, with their special insight and unique perspective that no outsider could ever replicate, may be permitted to do so. The process of diversity will be facilitated, it is believed, by having each group write its own, beautiful history, and then collectively read that history to themselves, thereby inculcating pride and loyalty to their community, and cultivating a smug sense of satisfaction that their history is clearly the greatest story ever told.

The crafting of identity-based histories has therefore become one of the most important and central sources for diversity policy

---

1 There are numerous examples of this. See, as one example, Dan Murphy, "Can Muslims write about Christianity?" *The Christian Science Monitor* (July 28, 2013) at https://www.csmonitor.com/World/Security-Watch/Backchannels/2013/0728/Can-Muslims-write-about-Christianity

and practice, and the debate over who gets to write those histories and who ought to read them and who has the right to question them is as complicated as it is confusing. If outsiders are incapable of writing the history of other people, since they can never understand those histories like an insider can, then what, for instance, would be the point of reading someone else's history? There would be no way to understand it, because full understanding implies an ability to write or narrate that story as well as an insider. Or maybe outsiders can understand just enough to know they were wrong not to admire the histories of those other cultures and identities, but never enough to question or critique those histories. Every culture has a nice story to tell, and if we collect all those nice stories together, we get the story of diversity, right?

Not even close. The main problem here is that not everyone has a nice history. In fact, pretty much no one does. Most of history is full of all sorts of embarrassing things that we wish would have gone differently but, well, didn't. This is something that lamentably unites all of humanity beyond our different identities: we've all been real bastards from time to time, to ourselves and to others. For far too long, the approach to linking history with diversity has been to rewrite history to erase the bad parts and blemishes and slurs so that we could all feel good about ourselves, the textual equivalent of the young woman's face in *Eyes Without a Face*, only with ourselves as the obsessed doctors and our histories as the victimized and blemished daughters. We want our histories rhetorically photoshopped, each one the written equivalent of a flawless model on the cover of a fashion magazine. But writing these bastardized histories that leave out the parts where we were bastards is just bad history, and that means that most of diversity is based upon bad history. And bad history, as it turns out, gives us bad diversity, full stop. The counterintuitive reality is that we need to stop writing these surgically sculpted and photoshopped feel-good histories in order to get a diversity we can feel good about.

The only thing that will give us a diversity we can trust is honesty, and an honest history is rarely, if ever, a nice story.

Looking back on history
I was once giving a lecture to a group of students on the interface between human rights and culture, and was discussing a few examples from South America in which indigenous peoples were engaging in practices that in any other context would clearly be human rights violations. In the context of human rights, for instance, systematically killing children because of their appearance would be a monstrous act, but since indigenous rights (as cultural rights) require states to respect and protect indigenous practices, even things like infanticide—for example infanticide that involves the killing of a second-born twin as a possible evil spirit—is often "excused" as a cultural practice of indigenous peoples.[2] As you can imagine, this creates problems. If the state intervened to stop the practice, it would be a violation of indigenous rights, but if the state did not intervene to stop the practice, it would be a violation of children's rights.[3] There was a tremendous amount of discomfort in the question-and-answer period that followed, due to the complexity of the situation, but at one point a student decided to simplify everything with a question I have lamentably heard so many times in so many different contexts: "Can't we just blame imperialism?"

I will have more to say about the historical topic of imperialism a bit later, but for now I mention this example because it shows how

---

2 Ana Paula Valentim de Araujo, "O infanticídio indígena e a postura do estado brasileiro," *Âmbito Jurídico* (2015) at http://www.ambito-juridico.com.br/site/index.php?n_link=revista_artigos_leitura&artigo_id=16393&revista_caderno=9

3 Michael Cook, "Indigenous infanticide sparks controversy in Brazil," *BioEdge* (September 24, 2008) at https://www.bioedge.org/bioethics/bioethics_article/indigenous_infanticide_sparks_controversy_in_brazil

deeply embedded the search for historical origins and historical blame is in discussions of diversity, and also to show how the unbelievably complex process of historical change is often brutally simplified to create easily digestible histories of the past upon which to build implausible versions of diversity in the present. History is deployed as a substantive justification for the majority of policies that are designed to create diversity in the present, and so it stands to reason that the quality of diversity we get in the present will be directly contingent on the quality of history we get in reference to our collective pasts. And so again, let me be clear: *bad history will yield only bad diversity.*

For those who aren't sure why or how history itself could become so controversial, I should clarify that when I speak of "good" or "bad" history I am referring not to the disclosure of events but more importantly to interpretations of how those events link together. It is not an instance of debating whether or not the American Declaration of Independence was signed on July 4, 1776. It is a question of *why* it was signed on that day, *why* it was written in the first place, *who* signed it and *why* they signed it, and so on. One or two generations ago, most American students were taught that the Declaration of Independence was signed by the Founding Fathers because they believed in the ideals of liberty and freedom and all sorts of other democratic virtues. Now, we have competing interpretations that question this more simplistic version. For some, the Founding Fathers were just one more group of DWM (Dead White Men), white privileged property owners who could not grasp the hypocrisy of writing about freedom while practicing slavery. Suddenly we go from a country founded on the principles of freedom and liberty to one founded on privilege and hypocrisy. For those who subscribe to the latter interpretation, for instance, diversity in the present becomes the project of dismantling all that privilege and exposing all that hypocrisy.

D. C. Zook

Debates about diversity quite often transform into debates about history. Conservative commentators eye critical interpretations of American history with disdain and suspicion and argue that they are undermining American patriotism by teaching current generations of schoolchildren that America was and is a brutish and hypocritical nation. They tend to see the American past with a sense of nostalgia and often decry the loss of traditional values. Liberal commentators, conversely, see these newer and more critical interpretations of history as more accurate and more inclusive for the rest of America—those who were not a part of that privileged group of white men who supposedly founded the country. They tend to see the American past as a heavily-distorted image of an America that never was, or if it was, was only for an exclusive and select group of elites. The American past was more myth than history, according to this point of view, and so re-writing a critical history of America that includes all of the identity-based groups that compose America in the present better serves the mission of diversity as it is currently construed. The main point here is to understand that whether one subscribes to a conservative or a liberal viewpoint, both efforts to rewrite history in a particular direction are equally biased projections of present-day preferences onto the past. That doesn't make them *wrong*, but it means we have to be well-informed consumers of those histories to understand the intention of both.

It probably won't come as much of a surprise that I find both sides of this debate to be engaged in their own peculiar brand of mendacious word-craft. While each side likes to claim that they alone possess the historical truth whereas the other side tells distorted fabrications to suit their political biases—"fake news" as it were—the truth is that all history is distorted. The key to linking history with diversity is not to eliminate the distortions—truth and history will *never* be synonymous—but to keep our distortions tempered with fairness. If history is the story of ourselves among others, filtered as it is through a chronological lens, then we cannot write that history one way about ourselves and another way about others—that would violate the principle of fairness. It is ethically inconsistent, for instance, to launch a diatribe against someone because their history shows that their identity-group participated in imperialism or genocide if one's own group shows the same. And it makes little sense to quibble over degrees of atrociousness: "sure, we committed a genocide, but the one you carried out was *far* worse than ours." As I have said before, genocide doesn't come in different levels of enormity. It's just an awful mess of one horror after another.

The fairness principle tells us that full disclosure—something known as honesty in other contexts—is the best approach. We cannot and should not eliminate the inconvenient elements of our histories, and we certainly cannot do so if we insist that others retain them in *their* histories while we surreptitiously eliminate them from *ours*. Motive and context are both irrelevant here. If we embellish or rewrite the history of a particular people in order to make that history nice, hoping to facilitate or enhance diversity, we will have in essence created a fabrication as the foundation for diversity. There are those who would argue that this is something we should accept in the short term, that we should tolerate the temporary re-crafting of "nice" histories for certain groups so they can feel pride in themselves and so diversity can be achieved. Once we get our diversity the way we want it, then we can go back and re-insert all of the blemishes. Even if I were to remove my brain, toss it in a blender, whirl it into a cerebral smoothie, and then pour it back into my skull through one of my nostrils, I would still retain enough intellectual capacity to see the foolhardiness evident in this approach. You cannot generate equal respect and understanding with unequal histories. I don't have a problem with telling the history of America in a warts-and-all format. I harbor no nostalgia for a traditional America and I have no interest in reading history as patriotic propaganda. But for history to play its proper role in the formatting of diversity, we have to tell everyone's history in exactly the same way. *Everyone's*. And yes, that means you, too.

Texting history
For those who cling to the erroneous assumption that history is just a collection of dates and names strung together in a chronological narrative, it is hard to appreciate just how much manipulative power the writing and re-writing of history can have on an entire generation or an entire nation.[4] For nations who view their history as a form of hagiography, for instance, to question that history is like questioning the veracity of someone's religion—it rarely if ever generates anything other than vociferous acrimony. One specific example of the power of history can be seen in the heuristic hullabaloo over the decision to issue a revised history textbook for use in schools in Japan in 2000, a decision that has since become known among scholars and analysts of Asia as the "history textbook controversy."[5] Though this was not the first time that a decision by Japan to alter its own history had created controversy—sometimes through the omission of events and sometimes through the alteration of single words (for instance in arguing that Japan "advanced" into parts of China in the 1930s rather than "invaded")—the instance in 2000 was the first time that a group of conservative-nationalist scholars had petitioned

---

4 This is a universal phenomenon. See, for example, Bilal Sarwary, "Why Afghanistan's past is being 'rewritten'," *BBC News* (August 18, 2012) at http://www.bbc.com/news/world-asia-18579315

5 Sven Saaler, Politics, *Memory and Public Opinion* (2006); Yoshiko Nozaki, *War Memory, Nationalism, and Education in Postwar Japan, 1945-2007: The Japanese History Textbook Controversy* (2008); Gotelind Müller (ed.), *Designing History in East Asian Textbooks: Identity Politics and Transnational Aspirations* (2013); Christopher Barnard, *Language, Ideology and Japanese History Textbooks* (2013)

for and received government support to completely rewrite a history textbook for adoption in Japanese schools. The New History Textbook (*Atarashii rekishi kyokasho*), as it was uninspiringly called, was designed to inculcate nationalist pride among young Japanese students by censoring out or otherwise altering unpleasant events that might create a sense of dismay or disillusionment among Japanese youth about the greatness of their own country. According to the conservative-nationalist scholars, Japanese history should teach Japanese students to love their country, not to question it.

Though only a very small number of Japanese schools chose to adopt the new textbook—less than 1% actually—the publication of the New History Textbook created a firestorm of diplomatic and popular protests in both South Korea and China. The governments of South Korea and China both issued official demands for Japan to withdraw the textbook from circulation, and mass protests filled the streets of cities such as Seoul and Beijing to denounce Japan for daring to rewrite its history in ways that would mitigate the crimes of the Japanese past, ranging from imperial atrocities to the use of Korean women as sex-slaves (often euphemistically called "Comfort Women") and even to the claim of historical ownership of islands and territories disputed by South Korea and Japan. In essence, these protests were claiming that Japan had no right to tell its citizens anything other than the brutal truth, and to do anything to the contrary, regardless of the motive, was unacceptable in any form and at any level.[6] Japan had to tell the truth, warts and all, and if the result was that generation after generation of Japanese students felt shame and humiliation at being Japanese, it was only because the actions of their country had been shameful and humiliating to others.

---

6 Mariko Oi, "What Japanese history lessons leave out," *BBC News: Magazine* (March 14, 2013) at http://www.bbc.com/news/magazine-21226068

Personally I think both ends of the spectrum create problems. History to create pride or history to create shame both miss the point that history is really designed to replace raw emotion with critical thinking. Does a young Japanese student really inherit historical guilt from the crimes of her or his ancestors? Should negative events carry the emotional burden of one's history, or do positive events somehow outweigh or provide balance? These types of questions, for which there are no easy answers, are precisely the kinds of debates that good history should generate. But lurking just beneath the surface of the Japanese textbook controversy we also find the sheer and unrelenting hypocrisy that saturates these moments when history is used as a platform for identity-building, especially when we circulate the histories of ourselves among others. Sure, China and South Korea were indignant that the Japanese government would dare to sponsor a textbook revision that taught anything other than the litany of degradation and abuse that Japan had inflicted on the world, but that indignation only carries weight if China and South Korea are presenting a truth-laden version of their own histories to their own students. And on that front, both South Korea and China fail miserably.[7] In essence, South Korea and China are denouncing Japan for doing the exact same thing they are already doing: lying about their histories to create nationalist pride.[8]

Revising history is like engaging in espionage: it's a bit awkward to accuse someone else of doing it if you are also doing it, too. To paraphrase the character of Captain Renault in the film *Casablanca*, when he is suddenly "shocked" to discover that

---

[7] See, for example, Stephen Evans, "Why South Korea is rewriting its history books," *BBC News* (December 1, 2015) at http://www.bbc.com/news/world-asia-34960878

[8] For a short and insightful summary of the history textbook wars, see "Textbook cases, Chapter 10," *The Economist* (July 5th-11th, 2014), pp. 26-7

gambling is occurring in the nightclub even as he is presented with the winnings from his own gambling, China and South Korea are "shocked" to discover that Japan might be altering its history to present a less-than-truthful account in order to serve the purpose of nationalistic education, even as they unabashedly do the same thing in their own countries. One would look in vain for any reference to an invasion of Tibet by the People's Liberation Army of China—instead, one will find references to "liberating" Tibet from Western imperialism and "civilizing" Tibet's own "backward" cultural practices (China plays the role of self-appointed imperialist civilizer in this context, though of course in this version Chinese imperialism is "good" and only Western imperialism is "bad"). In my courses, I sometimes assign an English-language article written by two Chinese scholars and published in an English-language academic journal from China that argues that the overwhelming majority of Tibetans are happy to belong to China and that they enthusiastically agree that Tibet is a part of China. Only a few bad Tibetans, whose minds have been "polluted and corrupted" by the Dalai Lama or other Western nations that are jealous of China's success, disagree, at least according to the authors. Amusingly, the authors maintain that all of the answers given to them by their Tibetan respondents were true and accurate because the researchers made sure that the Tibetans wrote out their answers under the watchful eyes of the Chinese researchers. (For those of you who have never taken a class in research methods, doing this would instantly invalidate the research results.) It is an article worthy of a hall-of-fame posting in the Epic Fail gallery of the museum of history, yet in China, it passes for peer-reviewed "scholarship" about China's history. Not even Japan's New History Textbook falls that low.[9]

---

9 The article is Zhu Yufu and Nima Zhaxi, "Freedom of Religion As Seen in the Liuwu Village in Lhasa," *Human Rights* 1 (January 2009), 23-28

South Korea has a similarly embarrassing record of passing off self-serving nationalistic propaganda as truthful history. Although South Korea has actively sought to locate and prosecute any Korean who ever collaborated with the Japanese during the era of Japanese rule in Korea (called *chinilpa* in Korean), a project that was revived as recently as the presidency of Roh Moo-hyun (2003-2008), history textbooks in South Korea intentionally obfuscate the general facts of its history to present itself as a country whose good aspects are truly Korean and whose bad aspects were created by foreigners. Japan is singled out and presented as a country that has been perennially hostile and aggressive toward Korea, and Korea is presented as a country that has always valiantly and heroically fought back. Complicity and cooperation with the Japanese are downplayed, especially when it comes to the foundations of South Korea's postwar economy. Most Korean historical writings in English are unusable for researchers outside of the country—I have never been able to assign any of them in my courses at UC Berkeley—because they are haplessly biased in the direction of Korean nationalism. According to Carter Eckert, an American scholar who works on Korean history and here referring specifically to Korean interpretations of its own history under Japanese colonial rule: "Any interpretation that lies outside the nationalist framework, let alone one that dares to challenge the relevance or validity of the framework itself, is often ignored as unimportant or castigated as morally deficient, regardless of the evidence."[10] And woe to the scholar who might actually present such an alternative or critical view of that nationalistic bias: it would be professional suicide in South Korea, and would most likely mean searching for a job at a foreign university and enduring permanent professional exile.

---

10 Carter J. Eckert, "Exorcising Hegel's Ghosts: Towards a Postnationalist Historiography of Korea," in *Colonial Modernity in Korea*, eds. Gi-Wook Shin and Michael Robinson (1999), p. 366

This kind of thing does not just happen in northeast Asia—it happens everywhere in the world, and everywhere it happens it leaves behind the stench of pathological prejudice. In Sri Lanka, where an ethnic civil war between minority Tamils and majority Sinhalese destroyed countless lives between 1983-2009, children in Tamil areas were taught to hate Sinhalese "oppressors" and children in Sinhalese areas were taught to hate Tamil "terrorists." Unlearning hatred in Sri Lanka will take at least a generation if not more. The same "Jewish conspiracy" theories that paranoid and mush-brained racists often spew forth in America, which are met with ridicule and disdain by other Americans fortunate enough to have their IQ stretch beyond single digits, are taught as fact in many Muslim countries as part of an ongoing campaign to cultivate an endless hatred toward Israel. The same countries that lambast Americans for being "so stupid" to think that what al-Qaeda does somehow represents all Muslims have no problem assuming that what Israel does somehow represents all Jews. In Turkey, historians and other authors who dare even to raise the possibility of the Armenian genocide can and often are charged with the crime of "insulting Turkishness." Imagine the collective atrophy of American intelligence and the slow descent into torpid stupidity that would occur in America if for example anyone who dared to raise the issue of slavery in America were imprisoned for the crime of "insulting Americanness." Suddenly plantation owners would reappear in American history as "agricultural labor facilitators," and Ku Klux Klan members who terrified so many individuals and families to force them into accepting their twisted hierarchies of hate would go from being advocates of hate speech to "motivational speakers." If you shudder at the thought of an American history that would look like that, then you are beginning to understand why we need to take history seriously in our discussions of diversity.

The history of America in America
It would be tempting to sit back and look at these examples from other countries and laugh them off as so much rhetorical nonsense, but the problem is that these types of initiatives are not just things that happen "over there." In the United States, debates over diversity have spilled over into the rewriting of American history textbooks and the revision of the educational curriculum in ways that often defy common sense and offend the dignity of all living creatures on earth, including humans. Starting with the assumption that American history excluded or somehow misrepresented all non-dominant communities, the history of America has been re-worked to create what is supposedly an equal space for all and an equally happy role for everyone in the story of America becoming itself. History becomes the fulcrum with which to lift the various agendas of diversity into our hearts and minds. The original history of America, it is alleged, was distorted to favor the dominant group of America, an elitist white cabal that had an interest in depicting all non-dominant groups in negative and offensive ways. A history that teaches the compelling reality of a diverse America must therefore reverse the damage done through these negative and offensive depictions. But this is precisely where the whole process goes horribly wrong. A new history that replaces negative and offensive depictions with positive and celebratory representations only repeats the same problem embedded in the earlier versions authored by elites and other dominant-group villains by adding in a new set of self-serving distortions that serve the interests of non-dominant groups. Instead of getting a clearer or better or more realistic history of America, we only get one that is distorted from a different perspective. In the long run, this is catastrophically destructive to the very principles of diversity that the architects of the new history purport to expound.

Consider first of all the controversy generated in the state of Texas over the construction of an entirely new K-12 education curriculum that goes by the name of CSCOPE. CSCOPE, incidentally, is not an acronym, which somehow gives it a nice Orwellian resonance—just to make the point. This new K-12 curriculum was created using public funds and was written and designed by a consortium of private educational service centers known as the Texas Education Service Center Curriculum Collaborative (TESCCC) (which therefore is an acronym, though not a nice one). The CSCOPE curriculum has been adopted so far by around 75-80% of the school districts in Texas, so unlike the controversially revised Japanese history textbook, which had an adoption rate of less than 1%, the CSCOPE curriculum has experienced widespread adoption throughout the state of Texas. There have been a number of controversies surrounding the implementation of CSCOPE, most notably that the meetings held during the period of curriculum redesign and implementation were mostly closed-door meetings, which meant they lacked the transparency and accountability that any democratic system requires. There were also controversies about the high financial costs associated with the adoption of the new curriculum. But those controversies paled by comparison with the heat generated regarding the content of the curriculum itself.

It didn't take long before some concerned parents and then many perplexed legislators began to hear some disconcerting feedback about what children were learning under the CSCOPE curriculum. One of the revisions placed in the CSCOPE curriculum, for instance, was that the perpetrators of the Boston Tea Party, traditionally viewed as patriots of American freedom and heroes of American independence, could justifiably be seen as terrorists, at least from the point of view of the British rulers, who controlled what was then the legal government of America.[11] In conjunction with other parts of the curriculum that offered revised interpretations

---

11 Eric Owens, "Ten shocking lessons a huge Texas conglomerate has foisted on public school students," *The Daily Caller* (February 21, 2013) at

of Islam designed to censor out negative references associated with the religion and emphasize only positive ones, the goal was to downgrade certain parts of American history (Boston Tea Party "heroes") and upgrade others (Islamic communities in America and around the world) to create an equalized, non-hierarchical space in the narrative of American history. In theory, a more inclusive and equalized narrative is actually a good and constructive goal, but as I have emphasized throughout this book, not if the goal requires censorship or further fabrications and distortions to what we already have.

Not surprisingly, the reinterpretation of something as hallowed as the Boston Tea Party, particularly through the invoking of a word that has been associated with the actions of one of the most hated and reviled groups in American history (al-Qaeda), created a lava flow of molten rhetoric from a number of different perspectives. Conservative groups excoriated the leftist, nay, communist (as they saw it) agenda of CSCOPE, and accused the architects of the CSCOPE curriculum of fomenting self-loathing and self-hatred among American students for their own country. And while progressive groups stood their ground and defended the changes as necessary for a new and ever-changing America, there was at least one delicious bit of irony that went unnoticed in the whole debate. One of the things that made the CSCOPE curriculum describe the Boston Tea Party as a terrorist attack was the fact that the Boston Tea Party participants dared to attack the "property of private persons" and, much to the horror of the CSCOPE architects, a "large quantity of merchandise" that was considered "valuable to its owners and loathsome to the perpetrators" was "destroyed." In other words, the allegedly progressive and leftist architects of the CSCOPE curriculum defined a terrorist as someone who would

---

http://dailycaller.com/2013/02/21/ten-shocking-things-a-huge-texas-curriculum-conglomerate-has-foisted-on-public-school-students/

dare to destroy the valuable private property of white, privileged colonial officials. Never before has the voice of the progressive left sounded more like the Tea Party, and here I am not referring to the original one in Boston.

CSCOPE eventually removed the revised version of the Boston Tea Party from the curriculum—at least they claimed they did—but the whole episode is certainly not an isolated incident in the contested terrain of American history as a foil for American diversity. In 2011, for instance, the attorney general of the state of Arizona, Tom Horne, declared the majority of Mexican-American classes in the Tucson school district to be illegal primarily because they promoted racial hatred and resentment.[12] There were other things that were troublesome for Mr. Horne as well, such as the promotion of the idea that much of the American Southwest should be returned to Mexico, but the main factor was the use of rewritten histories to promote racial solidarity, racial resentment, and racial division. Benjamin Franklin, for instance, was not so much an American icon as he was just one more white male racist, at least in the context of this "alternative" version of history. One could quibble with many aspects of this Mexican-American curriculum, in terms of both content and intent, and no doubt even minimal scrutiny would reveal a litany of poor choices that went into its planning and implementation. But there are deeper and more structural problems that require our immediate attention, problems that have to be remedied first— even before curriculum revisions can be implemented—to make history, and the educational framework in which it is embedded, work in the direction of a sustainable and constructive platform for diversity.

---

12 Marc Lacey, "Rift in Arizona as Latino Class Is Found Illegal," *The New York Times* (January 7, 2011) at http://www.nytimes.com/2011/01/08/us/08ethnic.html

One of the most crucial pieces of evidence we have for why classes like this are *not* constructive acts of diversity comes from *The New York Times* reporter who visited one such Mexican-American (or Latino) class during the controversy. Here is what he first observed, in his own words: "Although open to any student at Tucson High Magnet School, nearly all of those attending Curtis Acosta's Latino literature class on a recent morning were Mexican-American." This is precisely the structural problem we have with so many of the existing programs that claim to promote diversity: they neither promote nor contain any diversity at all. The specific structural problem we have here is that the class is full of Mexican-American students who want to learn about themselves rather than about others, who want to bask in the self-indulgent narcissism of hearing from a Latino teacher about how all things Latino are good and wonderful. The uninspired question we get in this situation, given the current uninspired state of diversity is this: shouldn't the state offer more courses in Latino history and culture, if it really wants to promote diversity? The answer to that is simple: no, the state should not do that at all. Instead, the questions we should be asking, based upon the very different premise that *diversity is about understanding others and not about admiring ourselves*, are questions like these: Why aren't there more non-Latinos in this course? Why aren't Latinos enrolling in courses to learn about Asians? Why aren't Asians enrolled in courses to learn about African-Americans? Why aren't more Asians learning Spanish? Why aren't more Latinos learning German? That's just for starters, but it does give the idea of how we are asking the wrong questions presently and why diversity is stuck in such a deep and noxious rut.

Compounding the problem is the trend that has developed under the current regime of diversity policy and practice to create "agency" among non-dominant or minority communities. Agency here refers to the creation or restoration of an active and empowered role in determining one's own individual or collective life-direction, in this case by entrusting them with the responsibility of narrating their own histories about themselves to themselves, with little if any oversight from anyone outside the group. To quote what former president Ronald Reagan once said in relation to arms control between the United States and the former Soviet Union, the best approach would be to "trust but verify." Instead, we are told for these newly-minted histories of diversity that we should merely trust without bothering to verify, and the result is a genuinely bizarre conflation of myth with history. Because "outsiders" who wrote earlier histories of these non-dominant and minority groups allegedly misrepresented those communities in negative ways, or so the general argument goes, insiders should be given a free hand to write a new narrative that "correctly" represents those groups in positive ways.

The Latino literature class that was visited by *The New York Times* reporter, for instance, began with a collective Mayan chant, apparently to show the deep and rich historical roots of all that is Latino and all that is Mexican, and apparently to allow the Mexican-American students in the classroom to imbibe the pride of their rich cultural past that had been occluded by non-Mexican historians. The problem with this whole enterprise is that in participating in these types of things, the Mexican-American students are just one step shy of believing in unicorns: the whole exercise glosses over the long and complex history of Spanish and Mexican exploitation and marginalization of ethnic Mayans, whose situation in present-day Mexico, in terms of racism and discrimination, is far worse than what Mexican-Americans experience in America.[13] But

---

13 See, for instance this report from the National Autonomous University of Mexico by Natividad Gutiérrez Chong, "En México, ser indígena representa discriminación, marginación y pobreza: Encuesta UNAM," *Boletín UNAM-DGCS-490* (July 23, 2016) at http://www.dgcs.unam.mx/boletin/bdboletin/2016_490.html

admitting that won't generate ethnic pride, and since ethnic pride is somehow seen as an expression of diversity—when in fact it isn't—those unpleasant facts get censored out and a new hagiography of self-reveling ethnicity is invented in the process. Even if the Mexican-American and Latino programs in Arizona do not constitute hate speech and racial self-segregation, as some opponents have opined, they do at least constitute a flagrant example of how current approaches to diversity fail. They give us an overabundant supply of mirrors to admire our faces when what we really need are windows to study the faces of others.

History and the present perfect
It might seem slightly irrelevant to argue about things that happened in the past and cannot be changed in the present, at least not until we finally discover some way to travel back in time and rearrange things so we end up in a different present. But as a reminder of what is at stake here, I offer a few examples of how disremembered pasts and other historical manipulations have a tremendous influence on how we situate ourselves among others in the present. In one of my classes at UC Berkeley, for instance, when I was discussing a research paper assignment that was required for the course and mentioned that non-English language sources were not only permissible but encouraged, as long as a translation was provided, one Latina student asked if she could write her whole paper in Spanish. The student, who was born in America (as I learned from a later conversation with her), wanted to write her paper in Spanish as an act of protest against an educational system that forced her to write in English, which she described as the "language of the colonizer." As she made this statement, several other students in the class showed their support and approval through one of the more annoying gestures that students have adopted in recent years: the silent finger snap (if you don't know what that is, I envy you). I replied that the assignment had to be written in

English, and also added an historical correction to her statement that left her quite flummoxed. Did she not realize, I asked, that Spanish was also the language of the colonizer? Her response to this, and I am not kidding, was to "correct" my ignorance by pointing out that Spanish was indigenous to Mexico, and since California was a part of Mexico before it was colonized by America, writing in Spanish was a way to restore indigenous justice into the present-day colonial system where English was "forced" as the dominant language. I shuddered to think of the layers of ignorant crust that went together to create this half-baked pie of self-righteous historical idiocy, much as one might react to a question from a student asking if Hitler was the president of America during the Vietnam War. I reiterated my point that English was the required language for the paper, but it was clear that this uninspired act of "protest" had given her an immense sense of self-satisfaction.

In another class, I was giving a lecture on Indonesia and was talking about identity politics in that country, pointing out among other things that citizens of Indonesia are required to list a monotheistic religion on their identity cards as part of their official identity. One cannot opt out and claim to be an atheist, since not having a religion is something that Indonesia associates with communism, and communism is a much-reviled ideology in Indonesia, particularly due to its association with the mass killings (of suspected communists) during the "year of living dangerously" in that country in 1965-1966. To accommodate the large Hindu community that lives in Indonesia, particularly on the island of Bali, Hinduism is categorized as a monotheistic religion, as is Buddhism, so that they constitute a "legitimate" choice of religious identity. One student then asked if Judaism was considered a legitimate religious choice in Indonesia, to which I replied that it is by most of the world but not by Indonesia due to its association with Israel. Indeed, for the purposes of identity, Indonesia only recognizes six monotheistic religions: Islam (the dominant religion), Protestantism, Catholicism,

Hinduism, Buddhism, and Confucianism (the last only since 2006). There is in fact a Jewish community in Indonesia, albeit a very small one, scattered mostly in Jakarta and Surabaya. The only functioning synagogue in Indonesia is located on the island of Sulawesi, after the one in Surabaya (on Java) was demolished due to pressure from anti-Jewish extremists in 2013. Since Jews cannot choose Judaism for the ID cards, they officially identity as Christian. As I pointed out in response to this question, they also tend to hide their identity as they face discrimination and opprobrium in a Muslim-majority country.

After the lecture, two Muslim students approached me and appeared to be upset. It was wrong of me, they stated, to claim that there was discrimination by Muslims against Jews in a Muslim country like Indonesia. Israel persecutes Palestinians, they said, and Palestinians are Muslims (which isn't entirely correct, but for the moment, let it slide). Since Israel represents all Jewish people in the world (also not correct), they continued, Indonesia's choice was an act of justice, not an act of discrimination. According to these students, I had given a negative impression of Islam to the other students in the class, and they asked me to correct this at the start of the next lecture. When I clarified that what I had said was factually correct, that Judaism was not recognized as an acceptable religious choice in Indonesia, and that Jewish people in Indonesia faced discrimination, the two students stated that it was not discrimination because there were not enough Jews in Indonesia to matter. In essence, since the Jewish community in Indonesia was a very small community, not recognizing the legitimacy of their choice as a real religion was not an act of discrimination. When I countered by pointing out that the population of Muslims in the United States was less than 1% and therefore also "small," which meant by the logic of their argument there could not possibly be any discrimination against Muslims in America, the two students pointed out that America was different because unlike the Islamic world, it had a long history of racism and discrimination. Once again, I shuddered to think of what twisted version of history they had imbibed for that statement to be seen as anything other than patently absurd. Incidentally, I never "corrected" my views for the other students, since there was nothing to correct—except, of course, for the perspectives of these two Muslim students, who had come to be believe that the history of Islam was nothing but one long unblemished tale of perfection. Anything that questioned that had to be wrong, and thus stood in need of "correction."

And then there was the Korean-American student who clearly had not prepared for the final exam in one of my survey courses on the history of contemporary Asia, and so instead of actually answering the essay question, she wrote an essay about how horrible Japanese people were and included a long list of historical crimes that Japan had committed against Korea. Incidentally, this was written in response to a question about democratization in Asia and so had nothing at all to do with the question. The student's essay could rightfully be seen as a racist tirade against Japanese people, but what I found truly interesting was that after the student received her grade on the essay—an F—she proceeded to contest the grade on the grounds that Japan really was a horrible country that had really done horrible things to Korea. When I pointed out that her answer had absolutely nothing to do with the question, and that her generalizations were in essence nothing other than a racist diatribe against all things Japanese, her response was that the things she said were true and therefore her answer was technically correct. How could she get an F for telling the truth? she asked.

When we have Latinos learning about Latino history from Latinos in a classroom full of Latinos, or Muslims learning about Muslim history from Muslims in a classroom full of Muslims, or Korean-Americans learning about Korean history from Koreans in a room full of Korean-Americans, we lose the one thing that makes history relevant to the present: a critical perspective. Remember—the number one function of diversity in education, at least according to the US Supreme Court, is to provide the "robust exchange of ideas," where different ideas are freely and openly shared among different types of people. With our current array of policies and programs, we mistakenly think that any curriculum that offers Latino history, Muslim history, and Korean history must somehow automatically be promoting diversity. But diversity always fails when it consists of ourselves among ourselves. What we need instead is a new curriculum that encourages or indeed requires us to engage ourselves among others.

On the borderline of history
At the Mexican border, there is no shortage of horror stories to be told. Racist border guards regularly harass those who enter the country illegally, sometimes extorting money from them and sometimes shoving them into overcrowded cells for an indefinite and miserable wait for a deportation that often turns into incarceration. Undocumented immigrants are exploited for free labor, due to their vulnerability, and women are often raped and sold into trafficking, if not by the border guards themselves then by local gangs or police. Whatever belongings they have on them are frequently stolen by the many groups of people who prey on their desperation, and the violence and racism they experience at the border should make even the most hard-hearted of people offer any and all compassion they can for the suffering of these people.

I have no doubt that on any given day, narratives like this one show up in classrooms, newspapers, and other media outlets all over the United States. But there is one interesting twist to the narrative I have offered here: I am not talking about the Mexican border with the United States, I am talking about the *other* Mexican border—the one to the south that separates Mexico from the rest of Central America. If you are thinking—wait, what?—then you are experiencing another moment where history and diversity clash in counterproductive ways. One of the things that is consistently muted in discussions about anything ranging from immigration reform to the championing of Chicano identity to the general idea of America's allegedly rampant borderland racism is just how much worse the situation is at Mexico's southern border—that *other* border, the one no one wants to talk about. It is difficult to sustain the argument that the border with America is definitive proof of how racist a "white" country is toward people in communities of color when the horror of Mexico's southern border shows that it is even worse in a "country of color" (Mexico). It would also undermine proclamations of things like Chicano Pride, often evoked in the context of standing up for a marginalized community in the United States, since the country upon whose heritage that pride is drawn is engaged in practices that make the American border look like a veritable human rights festival. I would never deny that there are abuses that occur on the American side of the border with Mexico, but it is a grave distortion of history to argue that the American border somehow reveals the oppressive, colonial, and racist traditions of America—especially if that revelation comes at the expense of censoring and suppressing any discussion of other borders (as hate speech, etc.). There is a reason that refugees and others who flee their countries in Central America don't stop in Mexico (unless they are forced to) and keep running until they hit the border with the United States. They know that no matter what happens when they cross into the United States, it will be nothing compared to what they have already endured at the other border.

    It is a depressing calculus indeed that compares the sufferings of different borders. And do take note that my point here is not to say that since the United States is not as bad as other countries, in terms of what happens at its border crossings, that the United States is somehow above criticism or somehow justified in the abuses that do occur at the border. But I do want to raise the question of why these types of details—of other borders—are kept out of the discussion altogether. So-called diversity advocates foam at the mouth when Donald Trump says he wants to build a wall (at the border)—another "clear example" of American racism against Latinos, they say—yet go silent when it is pointed out that leaders of other (Latino) countries, such as President of Mauricio Macri of Argentina, have proposed the same thing for their country and for the same reason. (Also on a side note, with all of the advocacy efforts in the United States to use the phrase "undocumented immigrant" instead of the allegedly racist phrase "illegal immigrant," in Argentina, the term "illegal immigrants" (*inmigrantes ilegales*) is used quite openly[14]).

Personally, I think building walls, whether in the US or Argentina or pretty much anywhere, is generally a bad idea, since they are the least constructive and creative solution to a complex problem. But let's bring the discussion back to the problem at hand. The main problem is this: the one-sided and simplistic narratives of history that are often covered in "diversity-related" classes tend to present only the positive aspects of the history of Mexico and other parts of Central America, while limiting the bad parts of the narrative to things that happened in the United States. This is what gives rise to occurrences such as invoking "La Lucha" (The Struggle) among Latino communities in the United States, as if struggling for justice was somehow something that only occurred after settling in the United States. It is the kind of historical and cultural myopia that gives rise to the suggestion that Spanish is the indigenous language of Mexico while English is the language of the colonizer.

---

14 As one example, see Guillermo César and Emanuel Fernández, "Superpoblación de inmigrantes ilegales en la Argentina," *Globedia* (August 4, 2009) at http://ar.globedia.com/superpoblacion-inmigrantes-ilegales-argentina

As I have said repeatedly, I have no problem with telling a warts-and-all narrative of American history—in fact I think this is the only acceptable sort of history to tell—but that project only works when we tell *all* histories in a similar warts-and-all narrative. If we do that, the question that puzzles so many people—Why, if America is such an awful, racist place, do so many people keep trying to find a way to get to this country?—is really no longer a puzzle. When we open up the narrative veins of our histories, we will end up with a very different and much more constructive environment in which to discuss borderlands, racism, and diversity.

Misappropriating history
To show how interconnected history and diversity are, and also to show how the discussion of diversity in America is itself intertwined with the discussion of diversity elsewhere in the world, I'm going to take you a journey that starts in the deep south (as in, South America), then makes a stop in Mexico, and finally returns us back to America.

Until recently, the story that Chile told itself about how the country came into existence was built around an idea known as *mestizaje*. The concept of *mestizaje* is that the people of Chile are the result of an historical mixing together of all the identities of Chile to create one separate, unified, national identity. Chilean identity is thus separate and unique, meaning in particular that it has no connection to Spanish identity. This explains how Chile could talk of being colonized by the Spanish but at the same time could detach Chilean identity from the violence of colonization, which was a Spanish thing and not a Chilean one. *Mestizaje* was thus an integral part of Chilean national history and national identity.

Right from the start, however, there had always been this voice, or more accurately, a chorus of voices, that tried to tear this idea down even as it was being constructed. The chorus of voices emanated from the many indigenous communities in Chile, most notably the Mapuche (the largest indigenous community) but also including several other groups as well, such as the people of Rapa Nui, which is governed by Chile. What the Mapuche and other groups were trying to point out was that *mestizaje* was a distortive nationalist myth and not an accurate record of what actually happened. In short, it was a denial of the historical experience of those who experienced the greatest suffering and exclusion in the making of modern Chile. The Mapuche, along with other indigenous groups, had seen their lands taken from them and their people displaced, in a long-term process that could only be described as coercive and violent. From their perspective, there was no mixing, no *mestizaje*. The colonizers didn't leave and go back to Spain when Chile became independent in 1810, leaving behind the separate *mestizaje* of the colonized Chilean people. There was no separation as they saw it. The people of Chile *were* the colonizers and imperialists, and the Mapuche and others were never "mixed in" but perennially kept out and subjugated by the Chilean people. Their histories were appropriated by the dominant colonial communities to erase and occlude the reality of lingering and persistent discrimination. After decades of trying to change the historical narrative of Chile to reflect this, in the last decade or so, Chile has started to get the message, and the word *multiculturalidad* (multiculturalism) has been slowly replacing *mestizaje*.

I mention this example from Chile because it gives us a new perspective on a similar historical narrative a bit further north. Whereas Chile has slowly accepted the painful process or revisiting and questioning their own national narrative, further north, in Mexico, things are very different indeed. Mexico's version of *mestizaje* is the story of the cosmic race known as *La Raza*. Like the story in Chile, the idea of La Raza blends the people of Mexico together as one race and separates that race from Spanish imperialism and colonialism, of which La Raza becomes a victim. As was the case in Chile, the many indigenous groups of Mexico, whose lands were taken by the colonizers and who faced and still face systematic discrimination and racism, have opposed and resisted this narrative right from the start since it basically erases their voice and erases their oppression from the national narrative of Mexico. Very much unlike Chile, however, their efforts to dismantle the myth of La Raza in Mexico have been systematically denied and rejected. This is why racism, which is not just prevalent but rampant throughout Mexico, is not acknowledged or addressed.[15] The myth of La Raza won't allow it.

Here is where we bring the story back to the United States, because there is a convoluted bit of irony at work here that only becomes visible if we know the background. Latino and Chicano communities in the United States celebrate and embrace the idea of La Raza. The law journal devoted to Latino and Chicano legal issues at UC Berkeley's law school, as mentioned in a previous volume in this series, is called *La Raza Law Journal*, for example. Latino and Chicano communities in the US certainly categorize themselves as people of color, communities that consider themselves victims of the systematic discrimination and racism of the dominant group(s) in America. Remember, too, from an earlier discussion that there is a deeply-entrenched belief among communities of color that people of color simply cannot be racist (only whites can be racist). Putting all of this together, you can see where this leads. La Raza communities in the US must deny the voices of the marginalized communities in Mexico that challenge the idea of La Raza because to acknowledge their stories of systematic discrimination and racism would blemish the beautiful and pure

---

15 See, for example, Ruben Navarette Jr., "In Mexico, racism hides in plain view," *CNN News* (November 20, 2012) at http://www.cnn.com/2012/11/20/opinion/navarrette-mexico-racism/index.html

history that the dominant voices of La Raza like to tell.[16] It would also turn La Raza communities, whether in the US or Mexico, into perpetrators of racism rather than victims of it.

To give a hypothetical parallel in the United States, suppose a movement was started to rewrite the national history of the American people. The people of America were then recast in this new history into one united group of people—let's call them Mericans. The Mericans were composed of a special blend of all the people in the US, including the Native Americans and descendants of African slaves, and all of these different groups came together and fused into the Merican race. *But wait,* a voice of critical opposition cries out, *what about things like slavery and the subjugation of Native Americans and racism and all that colonialism and imperialism?* That's easy, replied the master narrators of the story of the Merican people. It wasn't us. It was the true colonizers, the British, of whom we post-colonial Mericans are all equal victims.

I'm quite sure that there are many people who would gasp in disbelief at this retelling of American history, and quite justifiably would demand that it be exposed for the self-serving myth that it is. I know there would be many people who would do that because I would be one of them. But to bring this back to my original point for this whole chapter, it does nothing but harm diversity if we denounce the rewriting of the history of the Mericans but let other histories, such as that of La Raza or other communities of color go unquestioned and unchecked. Yet this is exactly what happens. This is how we end up with students in American classrooms demanding to write their papers in Spanish because English is the language of the colonizer while Spanish is the beautiful language of resistance for the oppressed and colonized peoples of the world.

---

16 Elena Reina, "México, frente al espejo del racismo," *El País* (June 30, 2017) at https://internacional.elpais.com/internacional/2017/06/29/mexico/1498692599_341796.html

Misappropriating resistance
If you really want to see an example of how diversity creates contradictory outcomes in which groups who claim they are marginalized end up marginalizing others and misappropriating their identities, then you need to look no further than the example of the *Ejército Zapatista de Liberación Nacional* (EZLN, Zapatista Army of National Liberation). The EZLN, more commonly known as the Zapatistas, declared its formal existence on January 1, 1994 in the southern state of Chiapas in Mexico. The date is significant as it was the day that NAFTA (North American Free Trade Agreement) came into effect. The Zapatistas in effect declared war on the government of Mexico, both for its participation in NAFTA and for its ongoing oppression of and discrimination against the indigenous communities in Mexico, of which the southern states in Mexico (such as Chiapas) tend to have larger populations. The most important point to understand here is that the Zapatistas were first and foremost a group dedicated to the protection of indigenous communities and indigenous rights. Remember that point, as it is crucial.

I can't tell you how many Latino and Chicano students have written papers in my classes on the Zapatistas (again, note how students almost always choose topics about themselves, never others). Yet, going back to my previous discussion of La Raza, an interesting thing happens in those papers, all of which universally praise the Zapatistas and express solidarity for their cause. In paper after paper, the Zapatistas are characterized as an anti-imperialist and anti-capitalist movement. To a certain extent, both of these claims are true. But where things get strange is when those papers claim that the Zapatistas are opposing US imperialism and US capitalism (the imperialism of US multinational corporations), both of which, the papers claim, oppress Mexico. It isn't just student papers where this happens either. Left-wing, progressive, and socialist organizations, in Mexico and the US and elsewhere, have also expressed their solidarity with the Zapatista struggle against US imperialism and US capitalist hegemony. Many an activist expressed their admiration and support for their *campañeros* and *campañeras* in the EZLN, as if to say "your struggle is our struggle, too."

Except that it wasn't. When the famous EZLN Caravan descended on Zócalo Square in Mexico City in March 2001, what they delivered was not a socialist manifesto against US imperialism and capitalism. What they presented to the government of Mexico was an Indigenous Bill of Rights. Many Chicano and Latino student groups in the US sent delegations to Mexico City to show support and solidarity—again, the your-struggle-is-our-struggle idea—yet the indigenous essence of the Zapatista cause was either ignored or else acknowledged but only as an integral part of La Raza, as if to reiterate that we all face the same (American) oppression together. But the Zapatistas didn't present the Indigenous Bill of Rights in Washington DC (capital of US imperialism and hegemony), and they didn't present it in Madrid, Spain either (capital of former imperialist power). They presented it in Mexico City, and in Zócalo Square no less—significant because Zócalo was associated presently with the current government of Mexico and historically with the center of power for the Aztec capital of Tenochtitlan. The only reason to present an Indigenous Bill of Rights is to make it clear that the rights of indigenous peoples are either non-existent or consistently violated. The only reason to present an Indigenous Bill of Rights to the government of Mexico is to make clear that the oppression of indigenous peoples and the violation of their rights are happening within Mexico. But if they are happening within Mexico, then who is carrying out the oppression and imperialism against the indigenous people of Mexico? The dominant, non-indigenous groups *within* Mexico, that's who. So now we have a conundrum. Either La Raza is oppressing itself, or else La Raza and the Zapatistas are separate entities, and the struggle of the latter is *not* the struggle of the former.¹⁷ Indeed, the struggle of the latter is a struggle *against* the former. But that conclusion undermines the idea that La Raza is an oppressed race, and hence, the Zapatista struggle is distorted or misappropriated by those who want to keep their history pure and unblemished.

There's another reason for this airbrushing of history in this context. Earlier I referenced the idea of what has become known as "500 years of resistance." The 500 years ago part refers to the arrival of Christopher Columbus and the start of European imperialism in the Americas. Even though at this point we are a little past the 500-year mark, we can still look at the difficult situation this creates if you are looking at it from within Mexico. Mexico declared its independence in 1810, but if there has been 500 years of resistance, against whom was this resistance directed after 1810? One possibility would be that Mexico resisted itself, but for obvious reasons, that gets a little awkward. Since the story of the arrival of Columbus was the story of the oppression of the indigenous peoples, perhaps the resistance was the resistance of the indigenous peoples against the non-indigenous ones. We're getting closer to the truth here, but we still have one problem. If the resistance really is the indigenous versus the non-indigenous (which is what the Zapatistas primarily were), then the situation in Mexico looks historically pretty much the same as the one in the US. But if that were the case, it would be nearly impossible to denounce US imperialism or claim oppression by the US, since that would now be confirmed as a cross-border shared history between the US and Mexico. This is where we find the idea of La Raza, the new race

---

17 Which is exactly the case. See, for instance, this story of how the Zapatiastas are moving into politics to change things *within Mexico*: Javier Lafuente, "El zapatismo impulse a los indígenas a las elecciones," *El País* (May 29, 2017) at https://internacional.elpais.com/internacional/2017/05/28/mexico/1496008267_211122.html

formed by the mixing of the indigenous and non-indigenous in Mexico, and a new race that is entirely and conveniently disconnected from Spanish imperialism, comes to the rescue. By blending the identities together and cleansing them of any imperialist residue, indigenous resistance is transformed into La Raza resistance. It isn't by coincidence that Día de la Raza is October 12—the day in which much of the Western hemisphere either commemorates or mourns the arrival of Christopher Columbus in the erroneously-named New World.[18]

The history of racism
It isn't just history itself as a general craft that needs to be reconsidered in relation to the role it plays in crafting diversity. It is also the various histories of specific topics that relate to diversity that need to be brought back under the view of a conceptual microscope and given a reexamination under intense and critical scrutiny. Among other things, history tells us the story of where things come from, so we had better be very clear about the origins of various historical practices relating to diversity if we are going to design a diversity in the present that addresses the injustices of the past and—hopefully—prevents those injustices from happening again in the future.

One specific and poignant example of this is the history of racism. We know we have racism in the present, so it is a valid and valuable question to ask where this perpetually offensive practice came from, in the hope of understanding how it came to be accepted by so many in the past and in the hope of dismantling and

---

18 Strange historical fact: while activists in the United States denounce the arrival of Columbus and seek to erase his name from pretty much everything (such as renaming Columbus Day as Indigenous Peoples Day), Costa Rica celebrates Columbus through its currency, the *colón*, which is named after him. El Salvador did the same until 2001, when they switched to the US dollar instead.

eradicating it in the present. The standard history of racism starts, not surprisingly, in the West, where we learn that in the mania of Western travelers and observers to categorize the world during the Age of Exploration and then during the Age of Imperialism, these Western travelers and observers sought to categorize the different groups of people they encountered, and the different identities they observed, and ultimately "race" became the preferred category to refer to different groups of people. That would make race a neutral category of description if left as it were, but when you then introduce the idea of hierarchy—of trying to explain the differences between groups in terms of level of civilization and cultural pedigree, for instance—you get the advent of racism. And when you add to that the idea of using science to show that the hierarchical differences between races, in terms of intelligence or civilizational status and so forth, is something that is beyond mere subjective perception and rather is an established and irrefutable scientific truth, then you slam head-on into the blunt and twisted juggernaut of what is called scientific racism. (As a reminder, in an earlier volume I discussed the manic over-reliance on science to "prove" that people were born gay—to reinforce the caution I advised then, note here how science was also eager to support racism and how people were eager to rely upon it as irrefutable proof of what they wanted to believe.)

So far, there is nothing in that history that is false. There is no need to dispute the history or rewrite it, except to finish the story and point out how the idea ultimately fell from favor and racism went from scientific and fashionable to idiotic and offensive. But if the story is correct as told, then what is the problem? The problem here is once again the same problem we almost always get when we blend history and diversity together: the problem lies not with the basic facts of the narrative, but with how they are interpreted. For instance, if we start with the premise that race is a concept invented in the West, we then leap to the conclusion—a misleading one, as I have already stated earlier, but one common in discussions of diversity—that only Westerners can be truly racist. If non-Western people appear to be racist, then only one of two things can be true, at least according to our current models of diversity: either there is a case of mistaken appearance, in which the non-Western person appears to be racist but is not, or else they *are* racist but only because they sadly imbibed—or were forced to imbibe—foreign (Western) ideas of racism. In the latter case, the task of eliminating racism in the world is conjoined to the putatively parallel task of eliminating Western ideas from the non-West to reclaim the indigenous, authentic, purified, and of course non-racist self from the taint of Western ideas.

The problem with this line of reasoning is in fact the line of reasoning itself: it is an untenable collocation of ideas that reads like an illogical train wreck on the express line to Stupidville. Just as I discussed earlier how the image of the "dumb American" refers almost without fail to the image of a white person (usually male), here when we discuss the origins of the related ideas of race and racism in the West, mainly Europe and America, we also think of them as ideas associated with white people. In other words, European and American ideas are by default white ideas, especially when they are bad ideas. But wait a moment, what about all of this new revisionist history showing that Europe and America were not just white during their historical evolution, that America for instance was composed of all sorts of different groups going back to the eighteenth and nineteenth century? If that is true, then surely the racism produced in America must be a collective project as well, right? If we are going to diversify merit, shouldn't we also diversify blame and guilt?[19] On that point of course, at

---

19 For an example, see Dara Lind, "Why historians are fighting about "No Irish Need Apply" signs—and why it matters," *Vox* (August 4, 2015) at https://www.vox.com/2015/3/17/8227175/st-patricks-irish-immigrant-history

least so far, the diversity activist answer has been a resounding *no*. Interestingly, when it comes to negative things like racism, no one wants to call attention to its diversity in American history.

Among other things, it is one of the many reasons we have identities that take advantage of what might be called the hyphen-of-convenience: to be Japanese-American, for instance, is to be Japanese-AMERICAN when it comes to claiming a role in the positive achievements of America, but to be JAPANESE-American when it comes to the American roots of racism. The claim of non-Western heritage, though born and raised in America, means that one can claim to be American, but in those moments when America is racist, since racism allegedly has only a Western cultural pedigree, then only Americans of European descent (aka, white people) are responsible for that part of American history. The hyphen is thus retained as something of a get-out-of-jail-free card for America's historical crimes. This practice perpetuates the idea that the guilt of America's past belongs to one group and one group alone, but the accomplishments of America belong to all. That idea is as impossible as the diversity that is derived from it. *Bad history begets bad diversity, and there is nothing that can fix that kind of bad diversity except good history.* In good history, we would learn that racism is just a Western variant of an idea that every culture has cultivated for similarly convenient and self-serving reasons that made sense at the time (and for many cultures that time is unfortunately still the present). If we write the warts-and-all history of discrimination and prejudice, then every culture in the world, and every culture in America, can easily be included. Indeed, it would be the most diverse history ever written.

Diversifying racism through history
One of the most widely-circulated pictures of America from the difficult years of World War II is the picture of a white man, a barber in fact, with a sign at the front of the store by the cash register

reading "We don't want any Japs back here...ever!" There were similar anti-Japanese signs to be found all over America at the time, and the problem that these created in America is that the proponents of these signs did not differentiate between Japanese from Japan, with whom the United States was at war, and Americans of Japanese descent, who were an integral part of America.[20] In better times, it would have initiated a discussion about whether or not someone who claims the heritage of a particular country can pick or choose which parts of that country's history and heritage they may lay claim to: can a person say they are of Japanese heritage, but only for the parts of Japanese heritage that are good and positive? If the answer is yes, then this might be useful in the present for a number of groups in America, including whites, for whom slavery could be disowned entirely. But in the period of wartime, the inability or refusal to discriminate between the Japanese in Japan and the ethnic Japanese in America led to what can only be described as a shameful moment—yet another one—of racism in American history. Not even war can excuse or justify that. So again, when we write the diverse history of America, I want that chapter included because I think it is important to document such things as they happened, in the hope that we can learn from those moments and collectively make sure that they never happen again.

So yes, let's be sure to include that chapter, as ugly as it may be, but here is the point: let's also include the far-less-documented chapters on anti-Japanese sentiment in Chinatowns throughout the United States at the same time, or the anti-Japanese sentiment among Filipinos and others in America whose home countries and heritage countries had been invaded and colonized by Japan. In Chinatowns in the United States, for instance, it was not uncommon

---

20 For a collection of similar images from the time, view the gallery at *Reappropriate* (February 19, 2014) at http://reappropriate.co/2014/02/11-images-of-anti-japanese-xenophobia-from-the-1940s-and-earlier/

to see similar anti-Japanese signs written in Mandarin, or to see signs in Chinese shops that said (in English) something to the effect of "I am not Japanese"—as if to say please do not discriminate against me but it is okay to discriminate against Japanese people and Japanese-Americans alike because I am angry at what they did to China. Isn't this also the same thing we see in the English-language signs in the shops of white shopkeepers? If we want to tell the history of diversity in America, shouldn't we tell this chapter as well? Shouldn't we talk about the diversity of anti-Japanese sentiment at the time?

And we need not stop with World War II. There is presently what I would call an informal anti-Japanese boycott in place in America among many in the Korean and Korean-American communities. These are people who scoff at the idea of buying a Honda or a Toyota or any other car from a Japanese manufacturer (even if that car is made in America) due to racial and historical resentment against what Japan did to Korea long ago (colonized it and annexed it to the Japanese Empire) or in the present (claiming territory that Korea considers to be Korean). Note also that in this mindset, for the Koreans who see things this way, the difference between being Japanese or Japanese-American is irrelevant—both are the same. In the 1980s in America, when Japan's economy was competing directly with the United States, it was not uncommon to hear Japanese cars referred to by various Americans as "rice burners," and in car-towns like Detroit or Akron, owning a Japanese car was a sure way to be excommunicated from one's circle of friends. This was seen as a racist practice by those who study diversity in America. So if Japanese competition against America was no justification for (white) Americans to reject Japanese products and indeed was seen as a form of ignorant racism, shouldn't we also see the current Korean-American stance against Japanese cars and other products in the same way? Isn't that a part of the history of diversity in America, too?

We could also globalize these kinds of histories and discover something even more controversial—that America is not exceptional. Granted, there are those who have always attacked the idea of American exceptionalism, as it seems to be associated with a certain type of arrogance, but when it comes to the more sordid details of American life, such as racism, those very same authors have seemed rather eager to let America remain as exceptional as it wants to be. In Thailand, for instance, in the years after the Great Depression (1929), many ethnic Chinese merchants refused to import or carry or sell any Japanese goods as a form of protest against Japanese actions towards China. The royal government of what was then known as the Kingdom of Siam (the name was changed to Thailand in 1939), pointed out that this actually harmed the recovery of the Thai economy from the Great Depression, and claimed that people who were truly loyal to the royal government would do what is best based on the needs of the people of Thailand, not based on what was happening in China. The royal government of Thailand, which had once sponsored the writing of a pamphlet that referred to the ethnic Chinese in Thailand as the "Jews of the East," in essence gave the ethnic Chinese in Thailand a choice: if they wanted to be accepted as part of Thailand, they should put Thai interests first, and conversely, if they cared for the things that happened in China more than what happened in Thailand, then they should go "back home"—or at least accept their second-class status as "perpetual outsiders" in Thailand, regardless of how long and how many generations they had lived there.[21]

In case you are thinking, "how sad, another Asian country forced to be racist by Western colonizers," then to remind you of something I pointed out earlier, Thailand was never colonized by

---

21 Kasian Tejapira, "Imagined Uncommunity: The lookjin Middle Class and Thai Official Nationalism," from Daniel Chirot and Anthony Reid (eds.), *Essential Outsiders* (University of Washington Press, 1997), pp. 75-90

a Western power. And what about that pamphlet calling ethnic Chinese in Thailand the "Jews of the East"? I'm quite sure that if someone had authored a pamphlet in America at the same time with a title like "Chinese Immigrants: The New Jews of America," we'd have no trouble calling it out for the racist tract that it was. So we have no choice then but to see the original Thai pamphlet also as racist. But then does that mean that Thai-Americans carry with them by heritage the historical guilt of Thai racism? Or again, can they claim only the nice parts of Thai heritage and history, and disown the parts that are bad or inconvenient? If the latter is true, then it should be equally true for all cultural groups (including whites), unless we want to build diversity on a shaky foundation of hypocrisy and double-standards.

The example from Thailand is just one example—we could fill volumes with those kinds of anecdotes, and quite frankly, someone should. We don't need to stop with the past either. I've been to many places around the world in the past few years where I have seen a wide variety of signs that show the experience of America is anything but exceptional, or is exceptional only to the extent that America has actually done something to act against these forms of racism. "No Arabs" reads a sign at a massage parlor in Bangkok. "Japanese only" reads a sign at a restaurant in Japan. "No Japanese" reads a sign at a restaurant in China. "No Americans served here," reads a sign at a shop in Seoul. If you are wondering why you haven't heard more about this before, it is because all of these things have been carefully censored out of history to make way for a conveniently one-sided history of diversity.

Why history is no excuse
I've conducted research all around the world, and while I can say that, just as in America, I've had the good fortune to meet some wonderful and inspiring people, I've also come across a fair amount of people who harbor some very ugly views about other people.

What I find interesting in relation to diversity is how the universal phenomena of racism and prejudice are treated differently outside of America, as if they are somehow understandable elsewhere, or not the fault of the people who harbor such views. The most common excuse offered as to why people who hold such awful views are not responsible for them is—you guessed it—history.

I once gave a talk to a group of Indian college students (in India), for example, who were preparing to come to America to enter graduate school. One of them, a student who was going to study engineering, asked me an interesting question about something he had heard about—something called "people of color." Was it true, he asked, that in America, Indians and Blacks were both considered part of the same group of people? Yes, I said. He was flabbergasted at this idea, largely because, as he put it, Indians had a far more advanced civilization. When I replied that such ideas could be considered offensive and possibly racist in America, he responded by saying it wasn't racist because he had been to Africa and seen Africans with his own eyes. It can't be racism, he said, if he were describing "facts." How could Americans not see this, he wondered?

Here is where history is invoked to explain the situation as something other than what it is. Because India was once a colonized country, colonized by white British people—people who can "legitimately" be racist—the poor Indian student, though he had never lived a day under British rule, has sadly been forced to internalize those racist ideas, and so rather than call the Indian a racist, we call him a victim of Western racism. The problem with this argument, of course, is that it is only accurate if all Indians are equally racist. That is certainly not the case, and indeed, at the event where I was speaking, many of his fellow students called him out for his views. So if it is possible to have the same history but end up with different perspectives, history cannot be the culprit. Choice must be involved.

Here's another example, this time from South Korea, a country which was not colonized by Western powers, but by Japan. In the summer of 2012, when I was in South Korea, there were some small demonstrations—quite small in fact, but at least they were there—against the government of President Lee Myung-bak due to one of his political appointees. The appointee in question had used the Korean equivalent of the N-word to describe the migrant workers and refugees from Africa who were in South Korea, and *yet was being appointed as the head of South Korea's National Human Rights Commission.* (The Korean word, by the way, is *kkamdongi*.) Hands down the largest number of complaints that the National Human Rights Commission deals with in South Korea relate to Korean discrimination and racism against foreigners, especially migrant workers and refugees, and yet here the government had no problem appointing someone who had gone on record to say how useless these people were—especially the black ones. I've stated many times that I don't mind a history of America that talks about the shameful acts of America's past—slavery and the racism that tried to justify it—and therefore provides a reality check for the idea of excessive American pride. But I also think we need to remember stories like this one from South Korea in the context of American diversity. Similar to what I said in relation to Thailand, if you are going to claim pride in Korean heritage, you need to accept the good along with the bad. Otherwise, if we allow persons of different heritages to choose selectively what they include in their heritage and history so that only the good things are included, then we need to do the same for all heritages and histories. A history of America with no mention of slavery? Sure, no problem. American pride! A history of Japan that glosses over the colonization of Korea? Why, of course—I insist.

The shameful history of history
So why do we have such selective histories that create such distorted views on identity that then end up buttressing a version of diversity that creates far more injustices than it redresses? Again, we have

to look to the practitioners of the craft of writing history to understand why so much of our history is so distorted and so much of it hidden away or buried under convenient excuses. If we go back to the example of Korean history, the reason that Korean historians would be reluctant to include a chapter in the history books on Korean mistreatment of foreigners is because those types of histories carry very heavy professional costs in South Korea. If you want to write a history about why Japan is the worst country on earth or why "Gangnam Style" is the greatest song every written, you will be rewarded with tenure and many other professional accolades. If you want to write a history about how Korean universities regularly violate international law by pirating American textbooks, you will end your career rather quickly or live in permanent exile.

The same is true of Korean-American history in the United States. If you want to write a history of discrimination *against* ethnic Koreans in the United States, you will be given all sorts of accolades by activists and professionals alike. Publishers will line up to publish that book. Such histories conform to current ideas of what diversity is, and so as long as you write conformist histories, all is well. But if you want to write a history of discrimination *by* ethnic Koreans in the United States, you will find yourself immediately under fire by professional colleagues, and you will be cast out of and disowned by the Korean-American community. Publishers will shun you and encourage you to "rethink" your ideas. The latter point also allows me to emphasize the point that most historians of Korean-American communities in the United States are themselves Korean-Americans, and so they have an incentive to write things in a way that brings them notoriety in their own communities as much as among their professional colleagues. The rewards are substantial to say what the community wants to hear and wants to believe about themselves. The punishment for doing the contrary—even if it is the ethical and right thing to do—is fierce and permanent. If you want to know why there isn't a book with a title like *Korean Racism: The Hidden Epidemic*, it isn't because there is no racism in the Korean-American community or because as a minority community Korean-Americans cannot be racist. It's because the professional and personal cost of writing such a book, especially by a Korean-American author (and it is highly unlikely that a non-ethnic Korean would be given the kind of community access to research something like this anyway), is simply too high. Better to leave that story permanently untold.

There are also those who might reluctantly admit to the pervasiveness of racism in all communities, but will quickly argue that now is not the time to talk about it. It is better in the moment to focus on the racism of the dominant group because it is the one that does the most damage and it is the one that is "worst" among all the other expressions of racism. Once we thoroughly document and then address and correct that one form of racism, we can slowly go back to the others to see if anything can or should be done about them. I have had many people at my lectures who have claimed we should not discuss anything other than dominant-group (white) racism as that might confuse the issue and dilute the movement for justice. If we only focus on one type of racism as a target, it is easier to mobilize resistance and defeat racism, or at least one version of it. It's hard enough to fight racism from one community, they say, so to open up a war on multiple fronts—that is, to fight racism as it exists in all communities—would be only that much more difficult and might possibly jeopardize the end goal of racial justice and diversity. Better to keep silent about the other racisms. Let's secure our simplified and grotesquely skewed victory against the one racism first, and only then go back to the others—maybe, if we have time.

I have a problem with anyone who tells me not to look at injustice in its entirety. If racism is a problem, and it most certainly is, then we need to examine and look at racism whenever and wherever it occurs. To return to a parallel example I brought up in another chapter, if there are two genocides happening in the world at the same time, I don't want someone standing next to me to tell me which genocide we should focus on for now—we'll save the other one for later, if there's time. I want to stop *both* genocides and anyone trying to tell me otherwise is a complete idiot. Similarly, if we want to end racism, we have to acknowledge all forms of racism, wherever and whenever they occur. How is one group's racism worse than another? Why not document and resist *all* racism at the same time? We do a tremendous disservice to the very idea of identity-based justice when we truncate the struggle to cover up the misdeeds and atrocities of our separate and collective histories, past or present. If diversity is going to provide justice for all, then we need to address all forms of injustice for it to work. If diversity is going to provide justice only for some, then quite frankly, diversity is not worth pursuing.

Why research on racism needs to be researched
There is no shortage of studies trying to show exactly what I just argued cannot be shown: that one form of racism is worse than others, often on the grounds that it is more pervasive or more prevalent and therefore should be targeted first. But nearly all of this research is skewed and flawed: most research is set up to reach a foregone conclusion, and most researchers working on diversity have a vested interest in promoting the interests of their own group. That is why we don't have Korean-American scholars hard at work documenting ethnic Korean racism in America—it doesn't further the interest of their own group. It is also why we *do* have a preponderance of Latino scholars working on the issue of immigration reform, considering that the vast majority of undocumented immigrants who would benefit from amnesties and fast-track citizenship programs would add to the size and hence the "strength" of the Latino community in America. What we get in the end are records and narratives from non-dominant groups, usually authored by scholars who come overwhelmingly

from within those groups, that document how those groups are engaged in the good fight to end racism (of the majority community), or how those groups are the victims of someone else's racism. None of the scholars and activists of these non-dominant groups are hard at work documenting how the racism of their own group is directed at others, or how hate-speech is just as prevalent in minority communities as it is in majority communities.

Take, for instance, the example of one common form of research that purports to show how one form of racism is truly more prevalent than others and therefore should legitimately be the sole target of efforts to create racial justice in the United States. A number of scholars take to the internet, which is sadly a bastion of hate-speech and racism, to try to document the patterns of racism that occur in various outlets and formats on the internet. One of the things that can be done is to look for frequency patterns (that is, to document the number of occurrences) for various words that are known to carry a racist intent or tone. There is no doubt that the use of these words is pervasive on the internet. The question is, how do we accurately document the existence of racism and hate?

Sometimes research about diversity and prejudice online gives us results that might make us question everything we believe about racism and prejudice, and more often than not, the response is to "re-interpret" that information to conform to the prevailing paradigm on diversity. A study by Kevin Lewis, a sociologist at the University of California at San Diego, that followed the racial preferences of users of the online dating site OkCupid found that the identity groups most likely to seek partners in their own identity groups were Asians and Indians, while the group least likely to do so was Whites.[22] But that result would indicate that at least some

---

[22] For a summary of the research, see Sarah Griffiths, "Does online dating reveal that we're racist?" *Daily Mail* (November 5, 2013) at http://www.dailymail.co.uk/sciencetech/article-2487684/Does-online-dating-reveal-racist.html

minority groups have strong racist tendencies and even more horrifying, that the dominant group is the one least likely to have racist preferences—both of which are, in the current state of diversity discourse, the *conclusions that cannot be reached*. What to do? Lewis came up with an explanation that brought everything back to the current orthodoxy of diversity: minority groups showed racist preferences, but only because they had lived so long in a racist society that they expected to face discrimination if they interacted with others outside their group. In other words, what appears to be racism among minority communities is in fact an expression of their racist victimization by others. Interestingly, the study did not show that these minority users were reluctant to contact only white partners, so if they feared discrimination, then they must fear it from all other communities, and not just from whites. One wonders how much longer we can get these kinds of results before we finally realize that anyone and everyone can be racist, regardless of what community they come from. Once we do that—indeed, *only* when we do that—can we speak of justice and diversity in the same breath.

To make the point more specifically, most of the research conducted to show that racism is prevalent is flawed from a number of different angles. I am not disputing the prevalence of racism online—even the most innocuous of word searches will turn up racism in a number of surprising and disturbing places. But deeply embedded in the internet are the words in other languages that are equally racist, but either researchers don't know how or where to look for them (in other words, if your searches consist only of English-language words and websites, you will miss 90% of online racism), or they do know where to look for them, which means they are most likely from the communities that use those words, but they aren't going to share the online location of that hate-speech and related racist content because, once again, it would mean being disowned by one's community for revealing what would be in essence a cultural trade secret.

Many communities bury their racism so that community outsiders can't find it, and woe to the person who starts trying to locate it, and even more woe to the community member who tries to divulge it to outsiders. To borrow a phrase from the tool kit of academia, until historians and other researchers locate and reveal the "hidden transcripts" of racism—that is, until they learn to read the coded language of all groups, dominant or non-dominant (see next section)—to locate and divulge racism and all analogues to racism, of which there are many to be found, we will always be only partially aware of why racism never seems to go away. There are those who argue that diversity is the antidote to racism, but this is assumed rather than definitively shown. We have a baneful and hideous cancer lurking amongst us in the form of racism, a social cancer that has already metastasized through the entire world. Yet somehow we want to look only at the surface, as if somehow, we could cure cancer with some strategically placed make-up.

Decoding the hidden transcripts of racism
Academics are both famous and infamous for inventing jargon and buzz words that pretty much no one needs, except for other academics. The best way to launch an academic career is to take something that any person can readily understand and then either make it completely incomprehensible, or else invent a haplessly convoluted descriptive term that only academics would use so they can speak in ways that exclude those they see as intellectually inferior (which for many academics is pretty much everyone else). So for instance, while normal people might "chew," in the world of academia someone will dream up a phrase such as "dentological mastication" and soon, other academics will follow, with the same determined gait zombies often use to follow each other in search of brains. Or while some people might just be pedestrians who "cross the road," an academic will coin the phrase "transportative pavement-centered ambulatoriness,"

and voila!—tenure is obtained. To be sure, not everything invented by academics weighs in as so much proctological fodder, and every now and then a useful idea will come along that also has the added benefit of making complex concepts slightly more accessible.

One such phrase that academics are fond of using is the "hidden transcript," a phrase associated with anthropologist James C. Scott and his work on how struggle and resistance occur in situations of uneven power distribution. What Scott was most interested in was the way that resistance by those without power could be discerned and distilled from the texts that we have, written as they were and usually still are by those with power. History as a text has traditionally been written by those with power—the power of literacy, or the power to censor and control content—and so rebellions and other acts of resistance are often excluded from the record so as to provide a more unblemished history of and for those in power. Scott thought a careful reading of those texts would allow us to recover what had been excluded, and thus the idea of a "hidden transcript"—things hidden from the public record by those who control access to the public record (that is, those with power), but which leave just enough of a residue for a careful reading to recover—would give us something of a better and accurate history by restoring to the record the voices and actions of those who had been excluded.[23]

Academics have always understood this to mean something that is employed by the downtrodden against elites: the underdogs deploy this tactic in their ongoing struggle against the power-elites. It's the story of good versus evil, a Spielberg film in the making, where those without power are good and those with power are evil. If we transpose this to the world of diversity, we have yet another way of seeing why people insist on arguing that minority

---

23 James C. Scott, *Domination and the Arts of Resistance: Hidden Transcripts* (1990)

and non-dominant groups simply cannot be racist: as non-dominant groups without power, their role in the story has to be the good guys. Since those with power are always bad guys, and since racism is also bad, then clearly only dominant groups with power can be bad guy racists. The relationship between history and diversity becomes the project of restoring the hidden transcripts of those without power—in this context, restoring the voice of minority groups to existing historical texts written by the dominant group (white people) to serve the interests of the dominant group. The non-racist minorities rewrite history to expose and ultimately dismantle white racism, and when the last chapter is finished, we finally get diversity, racial justice, and the social equivalent of unicorns leaping over rainbows.

The problem with these types of narratives is that they overlook a little thing called reality. Behind every bird of paradise, there is always a pile of *guano*. The premise that those without power are inherently good and their actions inherently principled, and that those with power are inherently bad and their actions inherently exploitative, is untenable and absurd. As I said from the start, we all have a history behind us, and few of them are as good as we would like to believe. So if "hidden transcripts" exist in one history, it stands to reason that they exist in all histories. And yes, one can find all sorts of references to racist and discriminatory actions in the histories written by and for the dominant identity-groups of history, but if we replicate this process and search for hidden transcripts in *all* histories, what we will find is that we all share a common historical trait: we try to hide what is unpleasant, especially when we know we are at fault. In the case of minority groups in the history of diversity in the United States, the role of the "oppressed" or "marginalized" is used as a filter to mask what is unpleasant *within* the histories of those groups. But if diversity is to give us a new society and a new history that treats all groups as equal and requires us to equally understand one another, then we need to extract out *all* of the hidden transcripts of our collective history. And that means outing the racism and the prejudice and the discrimination and the marginalization that exists in all of our histories. Non-dominant racism is therefore one such "hidden transcript" that needs to be restored to the narrative. You can follow a unicorn on its journey across the rainbows, but no matter how wonderful it might seem at first, at some point you are going to step in a pile of unicorn crap. And no, it doesn't smell like Skittles.

A hidden visual transcript: image from a Telugu-language magazine (Swathi Saparivara Patrika, 1994) in India, depicting life in urban America, as seen through the eyes of an Indian visitor; note the racist caricature of the black criminal

A *history of color?*

There is another irony that pops up in all of this that hopefully will put everything into a different perspective when it comes to diversity. Many of those who come to the United States from other parts of the world are those who benefitted generously from the many systems of discrimination that exist in other countries. That is, they come from privileged positions of status in society, where their privilege is based on a system that, if not exactly racist, certainly works in the same very ugly and very unjust ways. They would be, in other words, from the class that most others would see as the "oppressors," to borrow a word that is often used to describe the dominant group in the United States. Yet, though they utilized and exploited those systems of hierarchy and discrimination to get themselves into a coveted and privileged position to come to the United Sates, upon arrival, they are given the automatic status of "person of color," a category that implies that they have experienced oppression, though in reality they have meted it out to others. Eager to mask that unpleasant fact, they eagerly adopt the moniker "person of color," which all but makes it painfully clear just how pointless the whole categorization of history or society by "colors" turns out to be.

I'll go over some specific examples of this in a later chapter. For now, however, my point is simple: the "people of color" concept is a bankrupt idea that continuously drags us back to the issue of color when the point of diversity should be to move us *beyond* color. How bankrupt is the idea? Well, consider this: as anyone familiar with color theory knows, the color black is actually defined as the *absence* of any color, so by definition black should be the least diverse identity of all (and in fact could not be included in the category of "people of color"). Even more ironic is that white is defined as the presence of all colors, which would make white the most colorful and diverse identity there is. The very idea of what it means to be a "person of color" or to "have color" is based on the belief that there is a qualitatively separate historical experience between white and non-white, and as we have seen, that is a position that is untenable at best (the real question is why some people need to believe it is true). At worst, it ends up masking most of the injustices in the world behind a false dualism: people of color narrate a history of color that tells only of unidirectional injustice inflicted against people of color. The injustices that people of color have meted out to others are carefully excised from the story, or else the focus is kept only on the injustices committed by the dominant group ("white history"), as if those were the only actions that mattered. The latter tenet is particularly interesting: it implies that the things white and Western people do really are more important than what others do, which actually ends up endorsing one of the central elements of imperialism. And the very idea of "people of color" documenting what is seen to be the injustice of exclusion is itself an exclusionary principle: people "without color" are not welcome, so it mimics rather than resists the injustices about which it laments.

Everyone has a color, and if diversity is going to work, everyone has to play a role in that history. What we have now is a delusional belief that a person's color and qualitative historical experience are intrinsically linked and interdependent. But that idea is in turn predicated on an historical narrative of the world that is so full of contradictions it would make a Marxist blush. Once we retell that history and rewrite the book so that we all see what we have in common—the good along with the bad—the very idea of anything being "of color" will go where it belongs, in the proverbial dustbin of history. The swifter its disposal, the swifter we arrive at diversity.

Getting away with murder
I've said on several occasions that it makes no sense to compare genocides. They're all just uniformly awful, though each in its own individual way. As an example of the way that genocide extends its cruelty in ways that go far beyond just killing, I'll share a story

from the genocide that shook Cambodia to its very core between April 1975 and January 1979. When the regime that took power in April 1975, known to history as the Khmer Rouge (they actually called themselves *Angkar*, or "the movement"), they began to empty the cities and round up anyone associated with the previous regime. The Khmer Rouge cultivated a peculiar blend of ideology, partly built on ideas of Marxism and Maoism and partly built on ideas of racial purity. As the list of crimes punishable by torture and death expanded, and as the capacity of the Khmer Rouge to carry out their plans of extermination against enemies of the state and ethnic minorities became more aggressive, people tried to flee the country. Waves of refugees crossed the border into Thailand, where they languished in refugee camps, uncertain of the fate of friends and family who could not make it out.

The genocide came to an end when Vietnam invaded Cambodia in late December 1978, and succeeded in finally pushing the Khmer Rouge out of power in January 1979. Vietnam established an interim government, and initiated the process of trying to extirpate anything associated with the Khmer Rouge regime. Many people associated with the Khmer Rouge regime, the regime that had carried out the killings, saw this coming, and so they fled—to the very same refugee camps where their intended victims were still living. Survivors and perpetrators of genocide were now sharing the same space. To make matters worse, the former Khmer Rouge members who fled had already started their own narrative of victimization, blaming Vietnam for the killings and then turning to the very people who had fled from the Khmer Rouge, people who had seen members of their own families slaughtered by the Khmer Rouge, only to say: "We, too, are victims, just like you."

The situation is an outrage by any ethical or moral standard, and yet, to return to the theme of this chapter one last time, consider this scenario. If the United States were to send in a plane to accept Cambodian refugees for resettlement in the US (which actually happened), upon landing on US soil, the perpetrator of genocide and the victim of genocide now become equals as "people of color," incapable of racism, discrimination, or any other bad act (including genocide), victims of history rather than agents of it. This is the point where someone will usually ask, as I pointed out earlier, "can't we just blame imperialism?" And the disturbing answer is that many people will say yes, we really can just blame imperialism.

Is this really what we want out of history, something that allows the genuine bastards of history—the people who carry out genocides, the rulers that murder their people, the village leaders who sell young girls to brothels, or the extremists who slaughter and enslave others in the name of God—to walk on proudly and without a tinge of guilt because they are, after all, "people of color"? Diversity as we currently have it lets people quite literally get away with murder. Like the reference to the movie *Eyes Without a Face* with which I started this chapter, we seem willing even to overlook genocide and other historical atrocities to build a beautiful and unblemished history of color. If that's the best that diversity and history can do for us, then we are in far more trouble than we realize. We need a new way to look at ourselves and a new way to look at others. We need a new history as much as we need a new diversity. And we need it now.

CHAPTER 2

EDUCATING DIVERSITY

Nothing makes people hate diversity and everything associated with it like diversity education. It goes by a number of different names—diversity training, diversity curriculum, sensitivity training, multicultural education, and so forth—but what all of them have in common is their goal to educate Americans about the need for diversity. What they advocate is the need to move beyond the idea that America is just a white country with a few splashes of color here and there and to arrive instead at the idea that America is a genuinely multi-colored painting where no particular color is dominant. In theory, it means that America should be something like a Jackson Pollock painting, with all sorts of different colored streaks from every hue and shade imaginable all thrown around the canvas of America. In practice, however, diversity education simply paints different colored squares, each of which stands alongside the others, none of which are mixed, and the white square gets smaller and smaller in each repainted version, which is seen—delusionally, I might add—as a positive move toward a multicultural America. An educational endeavor that is supposed to tell us how we can all get along ends up being the most awkward and forced conversation imaginable. We mouth the lines during our "sensitivity training," but all the while we are gritting our teeth to get through it. For every hour of education we receive about diversity, I would estimate we spend eight hours recovering from it. But woe to the person who at any point has any questions about the presentation of the material. If the reality you see in front of you and experience on a daily basis does not match with the unrealistically simplified content that is presented in a diversity education program, the last thing you should do is raise any sort of objection or ask any challenging question. If you do, you will be told that you clearly need more diversity education. And how much more do you need? Enough to get you to the point where you stop asking questions. It's the closest thing America has to re-education through labor.

I understand that education should play a fundamental role in the process of crafting diversity. How else can we learn about and ultimately understand the difference of others without some sort of educational medium to help us along? My quibble is not with the need for education in the process, but rather with the nature of the material that is presented. Even the format is open to revision—not everything has to be learned through formal education alone. I am well aware of how the formal environment of the classroom can kill brain cells faster than a Bacardi 151 chugging contest, and I am also well aware of how lamentably undervalued are informal methods of learning, such as street-education, discovery through experience, and peer-to-peer interaction. Learning comes in a variety of different formats and through a number of different channels, and the key to using education effectively in the cultivation of a new approach to diversity is to develop a new approach to education as well. Since education is my bailiwick, so to speak, I can offer something of an insider's perspective as to how and why education—in my case formal education at the university level—fails badly in what should be a constructive process in crafting a new and dynamic form of diversity that works equally well for everyone, regardless of where they came from and regardless of where they are now. Not everyone experiences their diversity education at the university level—I get that—but the problems inherent in the university-level approach to putting education and diversity together are replicated in one form or other at every level of education, formal or informal. And when I say problems—oh my, are there problems. The best image I can conjure up by way of argument is this: if Diversity Education were a current student of mine, based on her or his performance in my class, I'd insist that Diversity sit in the corner wearing the dunce cap of shame, every single day, including weekends. If that seems harsh, well, read on, my dear reader, read on.

Reactionary radicals: diversity goes to school
Universities tend to attract or create radicals, though the meaning of *radical* is as obtuse and evasive as the definition of diversity. As a result, university-types tend to advertise their radicalness, usually by allying themselves with ideologies that also advertise themselves as radical. Radicalism, by design, positions its practitioners and acolytes on the margins of society, since if one is not on the margins, one is by default mainstream, and the mainstream can never be radical. Much like an alternative music station playing its own top 40—nothing like the most mainstream songs of all that is not mainstream—radical scholarship is riddled with all sorts of delicious contradictions, most of which we will not go into here. The reason I bring up the idea of radical scholarship, however, is that there is a structural and institutional reason that radical scholars often become involved in educational discussions on what diversity is and how to teach diversity to others. Since debates on diversity tend to focus on marginalized communities, and since radical scholars are self-positioned on the margins of the academic community (though in fact radicalism is mainstream at universities), there is a putative affinity between the two groups—the mutual

glance of awareness that says, "I know you and feel your pain." It's one of the many reasons that persons of color who are politically conservative take so much flak from academics—when you are on the margins, *of course* you would be radical and progressive, right?

But here is where things get really tricky. Diversity policies that are targeted towards marginalized communities are designed to end that marginality, which means that the goal is to take the margins and make them mainstream—in essence, to integrate. (As a reminder, the *Grutter* case on affirmative action I discussed earlier argued that the main purpose of diversity was to create an integrated society.) So, radical scholars and radical activists alike are always caught in an impossible yet self-inflicted conundrum: on the one hand they fight for the rights of the marginalized and downtrodden and fight for their right to an equal share of social access and institutional resources, but on the other they must do their utmost to ensure that their goal is never really achieved since when it is, marginality would come to an end and—horror of horrors—the radical would cease to be radical. Not to fight for diversity implies a passive complacency, but to succeed in obtaining diversity implies that one has accepted a position in the very system that you spent so much time denouncing as unjust. So radical scholarship aims just at the point in between complacency and success: the forever-fight-and-fail zone.

Now, a great deal of radical scholarship, and indeed much of academic writing in general, is pretty obscure and inscrutable stuff, commanding about as much of a reading audience as a self-help book to empower illiterate people. But over time, many of the basic premises that are built into these presumably radical approaches, though they become watered-down a bit, have trickled into what has become the orthodox approach to diversity education as it currently stands. While radical scholarship emerges from a number of different academic disciplines, there are a few things that all radical scholarship has in common. If I had to make a list of the fundamental assumptions that this form of scholarship makes, especially the ones most relevant to diversity and diversity education, it would look like this: (1) mistrust of power; (2) mistrust of elites; (3) preference for community-based and "grassroots" action; (4) sympathy for marginalized and oppressed groups.

On the surface, none of these is an inherently objectionable premise, and no matter what side of the political perspective you are on, there is much to agree with in these assumptions, broadly construed as they are. Even conservatives have a mistrust of power, which is why they tend to show a strong preference to limit the power of the central government to allow space for individual freedom. The problems and biases only begin to emerge when the details become clear. If we start, for instance, with the premise of a mistrust of power, and then we apply that to diversity and also give it a radical transformation, what emerges is the idea that power is to be mistrusted because power corrupts, and if power corrupts then those without power must not be corrupt, and since those without power are the marginalized communities, and since marginalized communities in America are communities of color, then communities of color are non-corrupt. To be non-corrupt is also to be morally pure. Conversely, to be corrupted by power is to be morally compromised, so if you are the type of person who fights for social justice—and radical scholars are obviously no exception to that endeavor—then you will want a better world in which the morally superior have power and the morally compromised either face justice or are pushed aside. In the world of diversity, the simplistic (but fundamentally flawed) assumption is that those with power are from the dominant community, "whites" to put it bluntly, and those without power are non-white, or "people of color." So how are the morally pure people of color to fight for justice against the corrupt oppression of the powerful white elite? The answer here is simple: by mobilizing communities of color at the grassroots level to radically resist the white privileged elite.

The alternative allows no alternative
There are many problems with our current approach to diversity education, dominated as it is by so-called radical viewpoints, but the worst among them is actually structural: the ossification of the curriculum over time means there is little room for debate and little tolerance for scrutiny. Anyone who has suffered through a program on diversity education has no doubt experienced the odd intolerance for alternative viewpoints in a program that is designed to showcase alternative viewpoints. It's as if diversity education already assumes it is providing you with an alternative viewpoint, so to question the alternative is to champion the mainstream, and since the mainstream is the problem, the only "right" choice is to accept the alternative viewpoint of diversity education without question. Progressives have already questioned authority, or so they claim, and so one cannot question the progressives. If you have any questions about that, then the solution, as I have pointed out, is to keep you circulating through diversity education classes long enough to make you stop asking questions. In doing so, we mistake acquiescence for understanding, which means that diversity education appears to succeed when it really just fails on a continuous loop.

Here, for instance, is an example of how diversity education exasperates more than it educates. I was once the faculty coordinator for a diversity workshop organized by a student group on campus with the laudable and idealistic goal of promoting world peace (sadly, they have not yet succeeded in attaining their goal). The student group had invited me to introduce the workshop, and then my role was to circulate from table to table, to participate in and help guide each of the different discussions on diversity that were taking place (each table had a set of questions to work through). At one of the tables, a female student who looked a bit unenthused about the whole affair mentioned in relation to her own identity that she was Costa Rican (born and raised in Costa Rica but attending UC Berkeley). When I responded to her statement with a question about whether she had experienced any pressure to identify herself as a Latina student, her eyes suddenly lit up: "Oh my God! Yes! I am so tired of this!" She then went on rather animatedly about how she had felt tremendous pressure—mostly from other Latino/a students—to identify herself as Latina, and when she insisted on just being Costa Rican, or on explaining how being Costa Rican and being Mexican were different things, she was derided by other Latino students for being "uppity" or in some cases just being "white." Her major complaint was that the Latino/a crowd on campus was dominated by Mexican-American students, who had the annoying tendency, according to her, of assuming that Mexico was the heart of Latino culture and all the other parts of Central and South America, including Costa Rica, were somehow quaint but mostly inferior variations of Mexican culture. While Mexican-American students complained that "America" did not understand Latino culture, she pointed out that the Latinos she had met on campus had no concept of Costa Rican culture and seemed uninterested in hearing about it. The main point was to get her to identify as Latina, because that would strengthen "the community."

So how did we get this point where, on a campus known for its prominent role in the Free Speech Movement of the 1960s, any talk of assimilation to "American" culture is treated as a hostile threat of the racist elite, but any pressure by Mexican-Americans to assimilate a Costa Rican woman to the Latino norm (as defined by the dominant Latino community on campus) is seen as a positive act of community building? And how did we get to the point where the one moment where this student finally felt safe enough to express her exasperation at identity politics on campus, was—as she herself pointed out with a bit of laughter—in a discussion opened up by a "white guy"? Over and over again, she had been told, by her peers and by other professors, that the White Man was always the enemy of diversity, that diversity was the act of rising up against the oppressor to fight for equality and justice. And yet her first moment of equality and justice came in a discussion with the alleged enemy and the oppressor. What's wrong with this picture? Everything, that's what's wrong. And my point in bringing up this example is to show how even at one of the most prestigious educational institutions in the world, UC Berkeley, one that is known for its championing of free speech and human rights, diversity education still ends up stifling any meaningful discussion about diversity. In her case, the pressure was to acquiesce, accept, and assimilate, all in the name of diversity.

I am going to identity three central examples of how diversity education ends up failing in just a moment. But before I do that, I should also preempt an objection that people might have to my discussion so far. The objection would be in the form of a question: why am I discussing and critically evaluating only radical or at least progressive (those on the political left) approaches? Why am I not also offering the same critical scrutiny toward conservative approaches to diversity education? It's a fair question and it speaks to the lexical poverty of discussions and debates on diversity. It's a simple debate indeed when only one of two positions is allowed: liberal or conservative. I haven't addressed the issue of conservative approaches to diversity largely because they are nonexistent on most college campuses (unless it is a conservative university) and the conservative approach is mostly to mistrust the whole idea of diversity as a liberal agenda anyway. When it comes to diversity education, it usually ends up like this: if you agree and acquiesce to what you are told, then you are liberal, progressive, or radical, whereas if you have any questions or show any skepticism, you are conservative, which means you are in need of more diversity education. The idea of thinking things through and making up one's own mind is like being Costa Rican—something that is mistrusted by all. Better to find a simplified identity label and stick to it. That's what diversity education tells us, at least so far. And that's how diversity education makes us diversely ignorant.

So here are a few trends and influences that have come out of the hallowed halls of academia, all of which have played a central role in creating the curriculum for diversity education, and all of which have played a role in creating a curriculum that generates more resentment that understanding, more tenure than knowledge, and more frustration than dialogue. Please enjoy the show.

Act I: Foucault said it, I believe it, that settles it
Nothing sends academics into an onanistic frenzy like quoting Foucault. On any given day, you can find an academic, standing at the podium of a lecture hall gesticulating and pontificating in ways that would give a southern Baptist preacher cause for envy, with the gospel of Foucault in one hand and an accusatory finger on the other. I sometimes think that when I see the bumper sticker that says "God said it, I believe it, that settles it," if I could cross out the word God and insert Foucault, it would sum up the last two decades of academia in a nutshell. The tragedy here is that the writings of Foucault are actually rather interesting and intriguing. The problem is what people have done with Foucault, to the point where the overuse of his writings and his philosophy has transformed academia into a caricature of itself. Perhaps a better bit of mischief would be to take the bumper sticker that reads "God, save me from your followers," and again, scratch out the name God and insert Foucault. That would be an equally valid complaint. So the question is, who is this Foucault and how has he played such a formative and—I might add—distortive role in the creation of diversity education?

As a reminder, I did discuss Foucault in an earlier chapter (in a different volume in this series), mainly in the context of his views on sexual liberation, which linked child sexuality to homosexuality. Here I am going to go into a bit more detail and focus on his tremendous influence in the field of higher education.

Michel Foucault (1926-1984) was a French philosopher who became one of the central figures in the development and establishment of what has become known as post-modernism. Anyone at a university will know that, because it is not really possible to make it through any undergraduate or graduate program anymore, except perhaps in the "hard sciences" (math, engineering, biology, etc.), without at some point encountering the work of Foucault. And I wouldn't say that is a bad thing either—encountering different philosophers and different ways of seeing the world is exactly what education should do, because it helps develop the life-skills with which a student develops her or his outlook on the world and charts their life trajectory as they move through it. But Foucault has become something of the bright sun that blinds those who read him to what else is around them, and Foucault has also become something of a dominant figure in the foundation of what has emerged as diversity education at the university. People have written troves of books on Foucault, so there is no need to summarize the entire corpus of his philosophy here. My interest is to show how the philosophy of Foucault has been employed to create a curriculum for diversity education that makes it all but impossible for diversity education to lead to diversity.

At the center of Foucault's philosophy is the insight that power, truth, and knowledge are not independent of each other. They are inextricably connected and deeply embedded in our everyday lives and social environments to the point where their workings have become invisible to us. What we accept as a concrete truth is really, for Foucault, a remnant or artifact of the process through which the dominant forces of society, utilizing the powers at their disposal, establish and secure their control over knowledge and ultimately produce the standards by which the rest of society accepts things as true or untrue, valid or invalid. Truth is therefore never absolute but always relative and always a by-product of the exercise of power. The general truth or truths created by dominant groups are referred to as "totalizing discourses," and Foucault, like all post-modern thinkers, has made it his project not only to show how these totalizing discourses are created, but also how they can be challenged. Non-dominant groups, for instance, over time produce micro-truths through the development of their own local and community-based knowledge, and these micro-truths complicate, frustrate, and ultimately question (the favored word among academics is "interrogate," which is strangely authoritarian and dystopian) the totalizing discourses that had hitherto determined their perspective on the world. The interplay, struggle, and strife between the totalizing discourse—the one that seeks to stay in power since it serves the dominant group—and the localized micro-truths of non-dominant groups—the ones that seek to resist, mitigate, or transform those dominant truths in ways that empower the margins—is the heart of social struggle and the essence of social justice in Foucault's philosophy.

If we jump-cut to diversity education, the links becomes evidently clear. Ideas such as the American melting-pot or the American dream now become totalizing discourses that conveniently serve the needs of the dominant white community. Increasingly aware of the inherent elitism in these totalizing discourses, communities of color produce a counter-narrative with its own micro-truths that ultimately breaks down the dominant narrative into something that, if the resistance continues long enough, will wrest the control of knowledge and truth away from the dominant group and create a new narrative with new knowledge and new truths for America. White truth will fall and give way to truths of color.

But there is a self-contradictory weirdness that lingers in all post-modern thinking, Foucault's work included, that undermines the whole endeavor in its entirety. Foucault teaches that we should not trust the so-called DWM (Dead White Male) orthodoxies of Western society, since they are the ultimate totalizing discourse. But that means that we should not trust post-modernism either, written as it was by other DWM figures (including Foucault). It is as if Foucault showed up at our party and said "Trust no one," except that if we accept his advice, we would not trust the person who told us to trust no one, which means we would trust everyone. So if Foucault tells us not to listen to DWM discourses that try to control everything, it means we need to reject post-modernism, too, which means that we *can* in fact trust those DWM discourses. Post-modernism never escapes the contradiction that it is itself a totalizing discourse, one that tells us to reject all totalizing discourses.

Confused? Amused? You certainly would not be the first, and you most certainly won't be the last. But, and here's the point as it relates to diversity education, somewhere along the way, those who control interpretations of post-modern knowledge, the dominant elites of universities, decided that a totalizing discourse that is self-aware of its aspiration to totalize was somehow magically exempt from its own rules, and so post-modernism in general and then Foucault in particular became the closest things the ivory tower had to a gospel, and faculty were the most willing missionaries any religion could ever want. Seriously, WWFD (What Would Foucault Do) bracelets would be perfectly in order here.

And yet, here is where it all comes back into the classroom in the guise of a post-modern aneurysm that replaces our active ability to think and with a passive compulsion to accept. Here's how it plays out: (1) since post-modernism explains everything, it is a totalizing discourse, and yet as a self-aware discourse, its power is legitimate and trustworthy and thus cannot be questioned; (2) since post-modernism exposes other dominant discourses as elocutions of dominant power elites rather than truths, dominant groups therefore speak untruths backed by power which means that non-dominant groups speak un-untruths, otherwise known as truths; (3) if those non-dominant truths could find a way to empower themselves, power would be taken from the dominant untruths and given to the non-dominant truths, which would then become dominant truths but remain truths nonetheless; (4) therefore diversity education should promote the micro-truths of non-dominant communities in order to undermine the untruths of the dominant community which have created so much oppression and marginalization; (5) since the promotion of these non-dominant truths will ultimately result in a society ruled by truth, which is now dominant, anyone who questions this approach to diversity education must be against the new truths and thus would be promoting the old dominant untruths, which is unacceptable.

The latter point, by the way, is a bit of preemptive post-modernism, a move that I might add is actually illegitimate by the rules of post-modern theory. The reality is that if communities of color succeed in supplanting the dominance of white truth (held in place by white power), so that we get a new dominant narrative, a new totalizing discourse of a "truth of color," then the first thing we need to do is form a new resistance that seeks to dismantle this new totalizing discourse, because remember, according to Foucault, all dominant discourses are to be mistrusted and dismantled. The moment diversity education succeeds is the same moment we must also try to make it fail.

It's enough to make George Orwell vomit with rage. But wait—don't reach for the chloroform just yet—this is just the start of things. For now, let us continue this fun-filled exposition into the foundations of diversity education.

Act II: Eurocentrism is dead, long live Eurocentrism
The generic label that came to be associated with every DWM discourse in the world, a label that was meant to convey the central fallacy in each of those discourses, was *Eurocentric*. To be labeled Eurocentric was the kiss of diversity death. There were many

reasons why anything Eurocentric was considered wrong for the world—it was even considered wrong for Europe—but the chief reason among them was that the Eurocentric interpretation of the world was also the imperialist interpretation of the world, and as we have seen previously, anything that was linked to imperialism was inherently wrong and inherently oppressive. Never mind that only a handful of countries in Europe actually had empires, and never mind the fact that American perspectives were also included in this sloppy and ill-conceived category of Eurocentrism—the point was that if it was Eurocentric, it had to be resisted and it had to be dismantled, shoved aside and pushed out of the way. Due to the power and reach of (European) imperialism, Eurocentrism had apparently come to distort every narrative on earth, *even the ones non-European peoples had written about themselves*, and so the distortions of Eurocentrism had to be "corrected" with as many non-Eurocentric narratives as possible. And since what was Eurocentric was assumed to be false, or at least distorted, what was non-Eurocentric—and here again we see this haplessly illogical leap of logic—was assumed to be non-distorted, and thus "true." Suddenly the Great Game was on: the good non-Eurocentric perspectives joined battle to supplant all of those bad Eurocentric ones, and the main force that had marginalized all those non-Western perspectives now had to stand back and watch the tables turn as non-Western and non-Eurocentric narratives pushed the now compromised and disgraced Eurocentric ones to the margins. It was time to marginalize the marginalizers, because as we all know, anyone who marginalizes others simply cannot be trusted.

One of the great ironies of this whole process was that much of the new material that now flooded American and European academia, material that showed how a world-perspective based on DWM—yes, those Dead White Men—was completely and inviduously mendacious, was actually based on the writings of radical scholars such as Foucault. Yes, once again, that's right: the person who told us that DWM discourses could not and should not be trusted was another DWM, one Michel Foucault. And those newly-radical non-Eurocentric histories and interpretations that flooded the market? Yes, they were based heavily on the writings of Foucault and other Western scholars of post-modern thought. The bad old Eurocentrism of the past, the Eurocentrism that was wrong and misguided because it was an "outsider" perspective and thus inappropriate for the rest of the (non-European) world—was supplanted by the good new Eurocentrism of the post-modern present. Even better was the fact that non-Western scholars, or Western scholars who were not white, if they imbibed and embraced this new Eurocentric anti-Eurocentric perspective, based as it was on a new generation of DWMs, could achieve the ultimate reward for resisting all that was Western: a well-paid academic job at a Western university. Eurocentrism was dead, long live Eurocentrism.

Now, at this point I am sure one could contend that this is just the sort of arcane nonsense for which the ivory tower of academia is famous. But in distilled form, these types of things do make their way into the general circulation of ideas, and in the case of the rebellion, or should I say "rebellion," against Eurocentric perspectives, this became abundantly clear in the evolution of diversity education. Take, for instance, Edward Said's classic text *Orientalism* (1979). In this book, Said argued that Western perspectives on the rest of the world had first of all gotten everything wrong, and secondly, and more invidiously, these Western perspectives had used the power of imperialism to force themselves into the minds of colonized and oppressed non-Western peoples, making them adopt and believe in an identity that was not of their own making and therefore not truly "authentic." The argument of *Orientalism* was based largely on the work of Foucault—actually on a misreading of Foucault, since Foucault would have argued that the resultant identities were not unilaterally imposed but rather a combined product of imperial power and anti-imperialist resistance (yes, for Foucault, we are always complicit even in our own oppression). But the general lesson that came out of the influence of *Orientalism* was that only Westerners had the identities they wanted, while the rest of the world was living an inauthentic life, forced to live that life through the nefarious agency of (Western) imperialism. And so the call to resistance, the call to reclaim authentic, non-Western identities, was on. Resistance in this case meant to reject the distortive influence of Eurocentric thought, based as it allegedly was on (European) imperialism, and recapture and reinstate the authentic identities that were lost by searching for the unsullied elements of the non-Western past and re-inserting them into the global present.

(Note also that when scholars and activists use terms like Eurocentrism and European imperialism, they assume that to be European is to be white, thereby denying the diversity of European history and society. Considering how many books are currently in the works to "radically" show how non-white European history and society has been, this will actually end up arguing that Eurocentrism and European imperialism were actually very diverse processes.)

Before I move on to discuss the allegedly new clear fallout of these efforts to set the world back to what it was meant to be (this theme should sound very familiar by now), I should point out—if you will indulge my spontaneous fit of knavish mischief—one wonderfully ironic example of how Eurocentrism ended up replacing Eurocentrism in what many academics still insist (*yawn*) was a radical transformation of the world. One example of a Eurocentric world-view would be something like this: to think of French as a global or "civilized" language, but to consider Arabic a regional or specialized language. With that in mind, let's take a look at the introductory page of Said's book, *Orientalism*. Here is exactly how it reads:

1.
The Scope of Orientalism

> ...le genie inquiet et ambitieux de Européens...impatient d'employer les nouveaux instruments de leur puissance...
>
> —Jean-Baptiste-Joseph Fourier, *Préface historique* (1809), *Description de l'Égypte*

But wait, you might ask, didn't I leave something out? Where is the translation of the French quote? Surely a book published originally in English would not just leave French quotes as is, right? Surely a book criticizing Eurocentrism and imperialism would not assume that French is a global language that needs no translation, right? But no, the book leaves the French just as it is, because *of course* an educated, cultured, and civilized audience would know French. As for the Arabic quotes in the book? Those are always translated because *of course* we would not expect anyone other than a native Arabic speaker (and perhaps a scattering diplomats and scholars) to know Arabic. French is universal; Arabic is local. So yes, that's right: a book that tells us to reject Orientalism and Eurocentrism is itself an Orientalist and Eurocentric text.

(Oh, and by the way, here is the translation: "...the anxious and ambitious spirit of the Europeans,,,impatient to utilize new instruments of their power..." Oh, those wily Europeans. The language of the quote is meant to invoke the language of Foucault, by the way.)

We can laugh cynically about all of this, but the influence Said's book has been very real and very profound. The curricula of schools and universities throughout the United States quickly became flooded with all sorts of new texts and new course topics—fiction from the non-Western world, and general courses on non-Western cultures. Especially at universities, the scramble was on to hire as many non-Western or non-white scholars as possible. On the surface, both of those things are actually laudable and wonderful things, and there is little to find fault with in the general premise. But the premise was not the problem. The problem came, as it almost always does, with the practice and the implementation.

The primary reason why diversity education generates so much resentment and why it does so little for diversity is that the curriculum itself is placed beyond question and beyond critique. The content has to be accepted, in full and without question, and not discussed. It cannot be engaged critically. Because this new curriculum was created as a corrective to the distortive influence of the Eurocentric viewpoints that had done so much damage for so long, they were assumed to be inherently truthful and hence beyond critique. If there was something to question and critique, it was Eurocentrism, and since all of these non-Western sources and courses were there to help us question and critique Eurocentrism, we were not allowed to question or critique them. Education is supposed to help us learn how to think critically, and yet all of a sudden, the new curriculum told us we could no longer think critically, unless it was about Eurocentrism and *only* Eurocentrism. If you were handed a work by Shakespeare, you could discuss it critically all day long, and if you could find a way to show that Shakespeare was Eurocentric, then all the better. If you were handed a work by Nigerian writer Chinua Achebe, then you had to sit and listen to how it showed that imperialism was the source of all evil in the world and how as an anti-Eurocentric text it was "true" and beyond question. (For the record, let me add that Achebe really was a tremendously gifted writer, and you should definitely read his works.) The fact that many of these non-Western authors, including Achebe, began to complain about how they were being forced to stereotype themselves into anti-imperialist or "post-colonial" writers who could write of nothing else did not matter. The new curriculum had an axe to grind, and that axe was aimed at Eurocentrism and everything associated with it.

The other problem that occurred as part of this new trend, a problem that was equally disastrous for diversity, was that in many fields, the new non-Western and non-white faculty that were so eagerly recruited were recruited as "authentic" representatives of their respective culture and identity. If you were going to teach Indian literature, then you had to have someone from India teach it. If you were going to offer African history or even African-American history, then it had to be taught by someone who was African, African-American, or at least black. And students quickly followed suit. If you were an Indian student, then of course you should study Indian literature. Chicano students were drawn to Chicano topics, African-Americans to African-American topics, and so on, and suddenly the great re-segregation of education began. No one was learning anything about anyone else, and everyone couldn't wait to learn all about themselves. Diversity education thus achieved an epic fail for diversity.

The fatal flaw in all of this, and it is a fatal flaw that *must* be removed for diversity education to redeem itself, is that the original assault on Eurocentrism, the assault from which everything else followed, got it wrong. Badly wrong. There is indeed a problem with Eurocentric thinking, but the problem does not arise from the *Euro* part. The problem arises from the *centric* part. Eurocentrism isn't the problem we should be addressing. *Self-centrism*, of which Eurocentrism is only one variant, is the problem. Eurocentric thinking is only a problem to the extent that it injects a European bias into the way it views all things. But all self-centric thinking is similarly biased and therefore similarly distortive. Afrocentric perspectives, Sinocentric perspectives, Latinocentric perspectives—all are just as biased and distortive as any Eurocentric perspective. Diversity education should not be designed to question and dismantle Eurocentric perspectives—it should be designed to question and dismantle *all* forms of self-centric thinking. And yet, look at what has actually happened: Eurocentric perspectives were pushed aside so that non-European perspectives could put themselves at the center of their own separate worlds. It's hard to get more self-centric than that, and yet this is what is still being celebrated as "diversity."

For one last point, let's bring Foucault back in, just for fun. Remember that Foucault argued that the truths around us are all products of power relations and power struggles, and that is as true for the macro-scale truths of totalizing discourses as it is for the micro-scale truths that challenge them. Like Edward Said, many a scholar has made the simplistic mistake of assuming that these micro-truths and the local knowledge they are based on are inherent acts of resistance against the oppressive truths of the totalizing discourses of our world. But micro-truths are generated by local knowledge in the same way that macro-truths (those that totalize) are generated by global knowledge. They differ only in scale, not in quality. Micro-truths in other words are generated by local power-struggles, and all power-struggles are contests for control and command. There is therefore as much resistance and oppression at the local level as there is at the global level.

Diversity education has spent way too much time showing how these totalizing and globalized truth-making and truth-enforcing discourses (such as Eurocentrism) distort the way the world sees itself, but has done so by erroneously assuming and presenting the micro-truths that complicate them as heroic acts of resistance and "true" histories. But non-dominant and local "truths" are not innocent truths. What we ought to be doing now, and what we should have been doing all along, is applying Foucault to these micro-truths and applying the same level of scrutiny to non-dominant voices. This, after all, is what equality demands: equal treatment. If we interrogate all narratives equally, we will see how the power struggles that create micro-truths emulate and adulate the macro-truths against which they claim to resist by following the exact same patterns and making the exact same oppressive mistakes. Afrocentrism and Eurocentrism, for example, are but two different servings of the same rancid dish. The Latino community speaks with one voice only if it stifles all alternative Latino voices. The gay community only becomes a community and empowers itself through the deployment of homonormative discourse. Eurocentrism is dead, long live Eurocentrism.

Act III: Telling white from wrong
The effort to push Eurocentrism aside was designed to make space for formerly marginalized voices, and as such was packaged and presented as the projection of power from the bottom layer upward, from the margins to the center, or from "the people" against the elite—post-modern populism, in a nutshell. After many years of effort, however, diversity has not made any significant strides, and frustration and resentment seems just as plentiful as ever. Rather than question the content and intent of diversity education, which would have involved considerable and valuable self-reflection and self-scrutiny, the panopticon eye of self-appointed radicals (the panopticon is a ruse borrowed from Foucault and refers to a dominant viewpoint from which power elites can view and hence control the disempowered) turned its attention outward. Somewhere, some unseen force must be holding back the ability of the marginalized and oppressed peoples to attain the power they seek, because even though Eurocentrism had been under retreat for years, diversity must still be operating under some sort of invisible cloud of oppression. But where could that cloud be, and where did it come from?

Before I can answer that question, I need to introduce yet another idea from the philosophical toolkit provided by Foucault and other postmodern thinkers. If you hang around a university long enough, or if you attend enough classes that are part of the diversity education curriculum, you will eventually hear someone say—through the voice of Foucault—that the most duplicitous form of oppression, and the most treacherous form of violence, is democratic freedom. I know, I know—you'd be thinking to yourself, "Wait, but what about North Korea or Zimbabwe? Isn't that far more oppressive than living in America?" Oh, but just you settle down your restive mind, because *Foucault and Friends* have an answer for you. Regimes like North Korea and Zimbabwe, they would say, rely upon the overt application of physical violence to keep control. We here in the West, in our seemingly safe democracies that provide us with freedom and autonomy, are completely unaware that democracy and freedom are illusions. The state has convinced us to believe in them, and so the state no longer needs to apply overt physical violence to make us abide by the rules. Instead, we police ourselves and convince ourselves that our belief in liberal democracy as a freedom-providing regime is natural and real and "true." This indirect pressure we exert on ourselves makes the power of the state invisible, and that is what makes it so heinous. Yes, the postmodern thinkers will tell us that we are "forced to be free," or "unfree in our freedom," because the normative power of the state, and along with it, of society, pressure us continuously to believe that we live in a state of freedom. The more we believe we are free, the more we are actually oppressed. We just can't see it or feel it because the sinister state, controlled by dominant interests, has convinced us that the freedom is real, and to the extent that we accept it as real, we are complicit in our own, vile oppression.

So wait, you might say, why aren't postmodern scholars fleeing this horrible, almost unbearable oppression and clamoring for teaching positions in more tolerable places like North Korea? Well, that's your first clue that most of this stuff is really just novocaine for the brain, because you won't find a single scholar who wants to leave this truly tragic state of democratic oppression. Instead, you will hear the answer that these scholars, due to their brilliant ability to see the oppression that ordinary people cannot see but tragically experience every day, need to stay put right here and educate the public about the dangers they face in this dangerous environment of so-called democracy and its evil counterpart, freedom. And part of that educational mission, of course, is diversity education. So what form does this idea take when we match it up with diversity education? What idea emerges in the diversity curriculum to show us what invisible oppressive force prevents us from attaining diversity?

Enter *White Studies*, stage left. (It would enter stage left because from the scholars' point of view, as the actors, they are on the (political) left, but as the next section will show, from the audience point of view, they are actually on the (political) right.) White Studies—sometimes called Whiteness Studies—is the diversity equivalent of the idea that our democratic oppression is invisible to us. Just as postmodern scholars, following Foucault, would argue that democracy "forces" us to be free even though we do not see the political forces that oppress us in our freedom, White Studies transfers this to diversity by arguing that we are "forced" to be diverse even though we do not see the racial forces that oppress us. As its name implies, the invisible racist force that oppresses us and prevents meaningful diversity from occurring is this duplicitous thing called Whiteness. Oh sure, you might say, you've seen all sorts of examples of white racism, ranging from police brutality to forced segregation to slavery, so we don't really need a whole field of scholarly inquiry to point out white racism. Oh, dear reader, how naïve you are. White Studies would point out that those are the visible examples, the examples that are easy to see. They are the North Korea or Zimbabwe of white racism. The truly evil part of white racism remains, like the invisible part of democratic oppression, persistently invisible to the untrained, uneducated eye. The surface-level racism that is easy to see is the least of our worries.

Just as postmodern scholars have to excavate the hidden layers of oppression and violence that exert their forces on us every day, because most of us are apparently too stupid to see them, White Studies scholars have to excavate the unseen ways that Whiteness continues to oppress and the many ways that white racism persists and entrenches itself right under our noses. The minute you think white racism is subsiding, that's precisely the moment when you know it is getting worse. It's just hiding somewhere, lurking there and waiting to find new, more creative, and more invisible ways to exercise its oppressive powers. In short, *whiteness is the enemy.*

If you think I am overstating the case, let me share with you another "radical" reinterpretation of a standard in the canon of classic American literature, namely, Herman Melville's *Moby Dick*. Novelist, writer, and Nobel laureate Toni Morrison wrote a short essay on Melville's novel in which she offered a contrary reading of the story that turned Ahab into the hero of the tale because Ahab tried to kill Moby Dick, and Moby Dick was, well, *white*. It wasn't just that the whale was white, it's that the whale symbolically represented whiteness. According to Morrison: "If, indeed, a white, nineteenth-century, American male took on not abolition, not the amelioration of racist institutions…but the very concept of whiteness as an inhuman idea, he would be very alone, very desperate, and very doomed. Madness would be the only appropriate description of such audacity."[24] In other words, we should all be so outraged at the inhumanity of whiteness as an idea that we teeter on the verge of madness in our efforts to destroy it once and for all.

---

24 The quote is taken from her Tanner Lectures delivered at the University of Michigan in October 1988. The excerpt can be found in Toni Morrison, "Unspeakable Things Unspoken: The Afro-America Presence in American Literature," *Michigan Quarterly Review* 28/1 (Winter, 1989): p. 15-18, or in the full text, found at https://tannerlectures.utah.edu/_documents/a-to-z/m/morrison90.pdf

White Studies is based on the premise that "whiteness" oppresses by its mere existence—intentionality need not be evident or present for the oppression to occur. Whiteness—which includes not just white people but also white imagery and ideas associated with whiteness (purity, goodness, etc.)—is dominant in spite of itself, in spite of any claims to the contrary. Take, for instance, the idea of a colorblind society, which at one point in time was seen as the desired goal and endpoint of diversity. The premise of a colorblind society is the erasure of race and skin color as significant markers of our individual identities. As visible and tangible characteristics of who we are, they would simply cease to have any meaning. We don't lose our different appearances of course, but the meanings attached to those appearances fade into irrelevance. From a White Studies perspective, however, we should reject calls for a colorblind society because it would only eliminate the surface-level forms of racism and discrimination but would leave intact the unequal and unjust forms of white dominance that remain invisible. That is, a colorblind society disempowers people of color because it allows white dominance to go unchecked, unquestioned, and unchallenged. The same approach can be seen with calls to move on to a "post-racial" America, which is also interpreted from a White Studies perspective as a surreptitious way of ensuring that white dominance remains intact.

All of this provides a convenient yet in my opinion illusory answer to one of the more peculiar aspects of the search for racial justice and harmony in the United States, which is the seemingly paradoxical way in which marginalized groups claim that the dominant (white) group is responsible for racism and yet those very same marginalized groups are the ones who champion racial solidarity as a method of creating diversity, even in the face of calls to move beyond race as a significant marker of identity. From a common-sense perspective, it looks hypocritical: why is it that the groups who claim to battle racism are the ones who also cling most stubbornly to racialized identities? But White Studies has an answer: it is because those marginalized groups know that "moving beyond race" is really a ploy for the dominant group to cling to power and to disempower all of the marginalized groups who might challenge their dominant position. Marginalized groups, the so-called "communities of color," therefore cling to race as a presumed act of radical resistance against the dominant group, because even as the dominant group claims to give up its racialized power, it only gives up what is visible, leaving the invisible elements of power in place.

The problem here of course is that White Studies really just ends up becoming a perpetual conspiracy theory, one that endlessly frustrates the chance for a dialog to move meaningfully beyond these separate and racialized categories. It's terrible for diversity, but from an academic perspective, it's wonderful: eternal conspiracy means years of research, and years of research means years of funding and years of chances for tenure. Again, this is why I rarely if ever trust "research" on diversity. Almost none of it is truly neutral or dispassionate, and almost all of it has an interest in prolonging the problem for the sake of professional profit. As a result, all of this academic nonsense bleeds into the curriculum of diversity education in a way that suppresses meaningful dialog and precludes the possibility of mutual understanding between different identity groups. What is presented as the pellucid peroration of so many perspicacious pundits is really just a cloud of hot gas that takes diversity nowhere. Like a flatulent assault in an elevator, it lingers oppressively beyond all hopes and expectations and prevents us from getting the one thing that those of us in the elevator want and need: a breath of fresh air.

Act IV: The conservative elitism of radical ("radical") thought
In case my assessment seems a little harsh, perhaps it would be a good idea at this point to offer up a very specific example of what I

mean when I say that all of the scholarship that purports to build a radical path to social justice really does nothing of the sort. Again, please keep in mind that I am not singling out so-called "radical" scholarship of the left yet somehow giving a pass to conservative perspectives—for all the talk of intelligence associated with higher education, universities are still locked into a conservative-or-liberal either-or dichotomy that resembles a kindergarten playground fight even in its more mature moments. I am focusing on the part that calls itself "radical" because they are the ones who constantly proclaim in a stentorian voice that they have The One True Path to Racial Justice and Diversity. In the previous section, I showed how and why the field of White Studies explains the peculiarity that those groups who claim to battle racism are also the same groups who cling most tenaciously to racialized identities. The claim of White Studies, as I explained, was that calls for moving beyond race as a significant or meaningful marker of identity were really just wolves-in-sheep's-clothing calls to disempower minority and non-dominant groups so that the dominant white group could maintain its dominance. Put differently, when a dominant group calls for dismantling race as a way to end racism, it is considered a *conservative* agenda in so far as the dominant group wants the power relations in society to remain as they are. When a marginalized or non-dominant group ("community of color") calls for the very same thing, it is considered a *liberal* agenda in so far as they are calling for an end to white dominance and a complete restructuring of power relations in society. So how can the same thing be both liberal and conservative at the same time? Short answer—it can't. What I want to do is to show why calls for "radical" action, though they sound cool (but not hipster-nihilist cool, which both hates and covets coolness), are just as useless as doing nothing at all.

I will do this through one specific example from one specific book. Andre Gunder Frank's book *ReOrient: Global Economy in the Asian Age* (1998) is not the best book on the topic and it is certainly not the only book on the topic. It is, however, typical of a whole school of thought that has combined past and present in a global setting with an eye to "correcting" the way history has run its course. It also informs the foundation of diversity education by engaging with the topic of the rise of the West, including things such as Western imperialism and Western dominance of the global economy. Parallel with the idea of the rise of the West is the idea of Eurocentrism, which Frank's book tries to emasculate in more ways than one. There have been many books before and after Frank's book that followed in the same vein, so this is just one example of what is in fact a whole genre of work that again, directly informs the field of diversity education. As for Frank's specific book, it is a text of revisionist history that tries at the end of the day to put the West in its (proper and inferior) place. I don't need to offer a spoiler alert, but there is a twist ending—so much of a twist that neither the author of the book nor those in the same "radical" school of thought saw it coming.

In a nutshell, Andre Gunder Frank's book argues that in a long-term, global perspective, the rise of the West to global ascendancy was just an aberration, an accident of sorts that happened partly due to extreme luck and partly due to extreme Western brutality and Western arrogance. For all the Eurocentric talk of the superiority of Western civilization, Frank argues that Europe and the West were pretty much the backward backwaters of the world for most of world history. The West, in other words, was the original Third World. The rest of the world was far more advanced, both culturally and economically. Chief among the other, more advanced civilizations of the world was China. Instead of looking at the rise of the West as an accomplishment, it should be seen as a "lapse" of non-European dominance, and according to Frank, "that lapse in dominance lasted less than two centuries." (p. 8) Even until quite recently, up until the moment of lapse, "Europe was still dependent on Asia…before the nineteenth-century invention and propagation of the "Eurocentric idea."'" (8) Europe was on the margins, while the "entire world economic order was—literally—Sinocentric." (117) Frank continues:

> Christopher Columbus and after him many Europeans up until Adam Smith knew that. It was only the nineteenth-century Europeans who literally rewrote this history from their new Eurocentric perspective. As [Fernand] Braudel observed, Europe invented historians and then put them to good use in their own interests but not those of historical accuracy or objectivity. (117)

I am partly bored and partly amused by Frank's observation that European historians invented history to serve their own vision of themselves. Gee, I'm shocked. What a *radical* observation. After I finish yawning I then feel compelled to mention, for instance, the story of Sima Qian, a Chinese court historian who was sentenced to death by the Chinese Emperor in 99 BCE (this was later commuted to castration) for failing to stick to the official interpretation of events, as seen by the Emperor.[25] The role of an official Chinese historian was to report and record only what served the interests of the Emperor and his power, not to report an objective truth or a critical interpretation of events. Yes—and I know this will shock no one—other civilizations have also invented historians and put them to good use in their own interests, and often, when those historians dared to disagree, they were snuffed out by their respective regimes. This happened everywhere, though Frank carefully censors those details out of his own narrative. Self-serving distortions of history have been the norm, not the exception. I find it

---

25 For more on Sima Qian, see Carrie Gracie, "Sima Qian: China's 'grand historian'," *BBC News: Magazine* (October 8, 2012) at http://www.bbc.com/news/magazine-19835484

very strange that this observation by Frank is considered somehow innovative or original or radical.

But I digress. We return to the regularly scheduled program by getting back to the main point of Frank's narrative, which is that there is good news for fans of diversity: the West is on its way back to the margins, and will return to the irrelevance from which it came, as the dominance of the global economy returns to its former non-European centers. The upstart and spoiled brat of the modern era, the arrogant West, will get its comeuppance, and the countries that were pushed to the margins by the inferior West will push back and retake their rightful and dominant place in the global economy. Justice will have been served on the plate of global history, and the arrogant West will be left begging for leftovers.

And hooray for that, right? Oh, but wait a moment, something does seem amiss in all of this. Actually, I think I should do something truly radical here. I'm going to put on my thinking cap—yes, I've had it off this whole time—and take a closer look at this argument. (On a side note, I can't help but point out the oddity of how so many Western academics continuously write that the West is the most horrible place on earth, and yet never seem to leave it.) If you are wondering if there is a Chinese historian writing a book about how China's current rise is really just a "lapse" in history and soon the West will return and push China down again where it belongs, well, that book hasn't appeared yet and never will—largely because any Chinese historian who would write that would simply languish in a Chinese prison or psychiatric facility (though as *Foucault and Friends* would remind us, that's nowhere as bad as the freedom to write what you want to write without fear of imprisonment or punishment).

Okay, but back to my main discussion. There's one other tidbit of information I need to share before I put together the answer key for this little game of "what's wrong with this picture." Andre Gunder Frank was, in his earlier academic work, associated with a school of thought in the field of political economy known as "dependency theory." Dependency theory taught that the West dominated the global economy, but it did so not by achievement and hard work, but rather by using its dominance to manipulate the global economy in a way that would ensure that Western dominance would be permanent. The rest of the world, the non-West, had in essence been shoved to the margins of the global economy, a place known as The Periphery, and had been reduced to supplying raw materials and cheap labor to serve the needs of the ever-growing and ever-dominant West, also known as The Core. The non-West had fallen and it couldn't get up, so to speak. The recipe to fix all of this was to document the ways that the non-West had been forced into a position of dependency on the West and then to find a way to break that relationship to allow the non-West to pick itself up off the ground and prosper, and of course to release itself from the exploitative grasp of the West. The Periphery had to rebel against the dominant powers of the Core by any means necessary, including revolution, in order for the marginalized and downtrodden to find liberation and independence. For now, hold that thought.

So, let's put all the pieces together and see what a radical perspective can do for us. According to Frank, the Eurocentric perspective on the rise of the West is simply self-serving propaganda that must be unmasked and exposed. In its place, he offers the (allegedly) corrected view that the rise of the West was nothing more than a "lapse" in world history, as Europe had really been nothing more than a marginal part of the global economy that for most of its existence was controlled by other, more dominant powers, such as China. Not only was Europe on the margins, it was also, as Frank himself points out, dependent on the rest of the global economy. But wait a moment, in his earlier work, Frank said that areas that were placed in dependent places on the margins of the global economy should rise up by any means necessary to achieve freedom and liberation. So if Frank's work holds any merit at all, then we should see the rise of Europe not as a lapse, but as a template for the first truly radical uprising by a marginalized region against the centuries-long dominance of China and other previously-dominant, non-European centers of power. European imperialism was really a rebellion against the iniquity of the previous global order, controlled as it was by dominant, non-European powers that wanted to keep marginal powers in the margins. Europe had to fight back by any means necessary, and one of those means was imperialism. (Remember, I'm not actually endorsing or celebrating imperialism, just having a bit of fun with the contradictions of diversity history.)

Is Frank, then, celebrating the European uprising, the template for true liberation, the global template for how to fight back against dominance and dependency and carve out one's own pathway to independence and freedom? Nope. In fact, as I have just shown, Frank is celebrating the return of the West to the margins and the return of the formerly dominant powers to their rightfully dominant places. The revolution from the margins, the "lapse" in the way the world *should* have been, if those troublesome Europeans hadn't fought back and (temporarily) changed things, has been soundly defeated and power has been restored to the centers who rightly held it for so long. And Frank couldn't be happier.

Except that there is one glaring error in all of this: *Frank's vision, and all visions like it, is as conservative and reactionary as one can get.* "Radical" history turns out to be reactionary history. What Frank is celebrating is the failure of the West's revolution to change its position from the margins and from the periphery, just as he is celebrating the return to power of all those dominant forces that were temporarily ousted by the uprising from the oppressed and marginalized. The elites of the global economy suffered a shock, but thankfully it was only a temporary one, a lapse in the status quo, caused by those troublesome Westerners. Now that it looks like the uprising has failed, we can all breathe a conservative sigh of relief as the traditional elites once again return to power. If you are still not seeing the problem, then just for some rakish mischief, let's now transpose this "radical" story onto diversity education in America. Here is how the story would go.

After having dominated American life for so long—economically, socially, politically and culturally—the dominant white community has faced an ever-growing threat from the margins. Communities of color, deploying their self-serving histories, have made a bid for power to unseat the dominant community and indeed, to push it to the margins. And the white community has indeed suffered a setback in its power, and those troublesome marginalized communities—why, it's like the barbarians are at the gate—have found a way to take things over. Yes, they have their self-serving propaganda, in the form of political correctness and racialized justice, but fortunately there are signs that the revolution is failing, that the marginalized communities have had their day but are now receding back to the margins where they belong. And soon the dominant white elites will return to power, as it should be and always will be—those that once ruled always should rule, according to Frank and others like him—and true justice will be restored. The threat from the margins will have been squashed, the lapse in white power will be reversed, and the marginalized peoples will have been taught a humbling lesson: never challenge the way things are.

So there it is, your "radical" vision of diversity. And incidentally, if that *is* your radical vision of diversity, then I've got some good news for you: the KKK called, and they've got an extra hood with your name written all over it.

Who can tell me who I am?
Have you ever walked into an Indian restaurant and discovered that the cook and the wait-staff were white, and suddenly had second

thoughts? You find yourself thinking—This can't be authentic, can it? Have you ever walked into a Chinese restaurant and discovered that the cooks and the wait-staff were Mexican, and thought the same thing? Or have you walked into a Mexican restaurant with a Chinese cook and wait-staff, and again, thought the same? Or perhaps you took a Tai-Chi class taught by a white woman from Wyoming and somehow felt uneasy, wishing the instructor were Chinese instead. Or alternatively, perhaps you took a yoga class and found that the instructor was from India and so thought you were in for some special, authentic knowledge—it just *had* to be a good class, with all that native Indian wisdom. Or maybe you took a class on how to make barbecue, and when two dudes from Texas dressed like cowboys, Tex and his partner Co-Tex, walked in, complete with deep Texas accents, you just knew you were going to learn barbecue the right, authentic way.

If you answered yes to any of those questions, or could think of similar situations where you had a similar reaction, then I have one more question for you: have you ever heard Yo-Yo Ma play the cello? Ma is considered one of the finest cellists in the world—an assessment with which I certainly agree—and yet, if you answered any of the questions I just asked in the affirmative, you would struggle to find a way to reconcile the image of an ethnic Chinese person (incidentally he was born in Paris to Chinese parents) mastering a Western instrument better than a more "authentically" Western person. Wouldn't a white person just be innately better at picking up the cello? The answer, of course, is that thinking this way is absolute nonsense. This is where, once again, I have to take aim at the self-appointed crusaders against cultural appropriation. If we accept their viewpoint, then we have to turn to Yo-Yo Ma and tell him, in the words of a website I quoted earlier, STOP TRYING TO BE OTHER CULTURES! A Chinese person needs to stick to Chinese instruments, and Yo-Yo Ma's unbelievable talent on the cello is really just "inauthentic" noise. I've said if before and I'll say it again: *cultural appropriation is a necessary and essential part of diversity.* Diversity cannot succeed without it.

It doesn't take a Western, white person to master an instrument invented by Western white people. Anyone can master the cello, just as any citizen of Mexico can master Chinese cooking, and any white woman from Wyoming can master Tai-Chi. The converse is also true. Indian cooks can make horrible Indian food, and white Western people can genuinely suck at playing cello (sadly, I know some of them). Not everyone in China just "knows" how to do Tai-Chi. The idea that cultural knowledge is intrinsic in our very being, that Spanish people automatically make better paella than anyone else, for instance, is a dangerous idea, one that borders on racism. And yet—and here is the truly sad part—it is an idea that has been embraced by the very idea of diversity education. In a way, diversity education actually teaches us to be *more* racist, not less. It's time for another round of that famous children's game: what's wrong with this picture?

A few years ago, I attended one of the many cultural festivals that are held in Berkeley throughout the year. This one happened to be a festival that was devoted to the cultures of India, and like most cultural festivals, it featured food stalls with food from the region, arts and crafts from the region for sale, various workshops to learn about the cultures from the region, and of course cultural performances throughout the day. One of those cultural performances was to feature an exhibition of Bharatanatyam dancing, a complex and intricate and intricately beautiful form of dancing with its historical and cultural origins in southern India. The festival organizers had contacted a local teacher who had studied for many years in India and had a local dance studio, and asked her to set up the exhibition dance performance. She did so, and brought along her best students to perform the dancing while she explained what was going on—the various moves and gestures, the story being told through the movement of the dancer, and so forth. There is one more bit of information I need to share at this point, and that is that the woman was a white American woman and some of her best students were white as well. So the dance performance had both white and Indian-heritage students dancing while a white woman explained each of the moves and gestures.

As soon as the dance exhibition started, a small group of people left to go in search of the festival organizers with one question in search of an answer: Why was a white woman leading this dance performance when there were so many Indian people who could have done so? And why were there white dancers performing Bharatanatyam? In a cultural exhibition, only those from the culture should be exhibiting the dance. One of them went so far as to say that the sight of white people doing Bharatanatyam might give the wrong idea to the Indian children who were present.

Is this racist? As they say in Minnesota—oh, you betcha. The idea that it would be better for an Indian child to perform the dance poorly than for a white child to do so flawlessly is offensively absurd, and yet diversity education and diversity policy, as currently practiced, seems to think this is exactly what we should do. The reason for this can be traced, once again, to the idea that Eurocentrism somehow spoiled the whole world. Since Eurocentrism is an affliction that seems to be inherent in all white Western people (interestingly, non-white Westerners are immune from this), and since Eurocentrism is responsible for all of the negative and biased and distorted images of all non-Western peoples, then diversity, in its mission to correct all histories of the past and free them from bias in the present, has deemed it necessary to expunge the Eurocentric taint from the record. What that means is that cultural learning, cultural transmission, cultural teaching and pretty much anything relating to the non-Western world has to be "diversified," which in this case means making sure that white Westerners are not involved *and* making sure that "cultural natives" hold a monopoly on their own cultural information. But since we know from the previous section that it isn't the Euro part of Eurocentrism that is the problem but rather the centric part, putting cultural information into the hands of those who champion their own cultures only gives us more ethno-centrism. In other words, this practice does not correct or resist Eurocentrism so much as it replicates and emulates it. We are diversifying the lack of diversity.

In essence, what diversity education has done is re-segregate culture, and in fact re-segregate all of society by categories of identity. By appointing the members of specific groups as automatic experts in their own culture by mere virtue of innate membership, we create exclusive enclaves that shut down meaningful intercultural understanding and interaction. This is a *really* bad idea. For one thing, it mistakes familiarity with knowledge, when the two are very different and quite distinct. Indeed, it mistakes appearance with knowledge. This is why we think we should see Indians cooking in an Indian restaurant, even if the food is bad, and have a hard time coming to terms with an Italian chef (for instance) making Indian food better than an Indian. This is also why we end up with these bizarre trends in all levels of the American education system where we feel compelled to defer to or hire "native experts" for anything that relates to something that is non-Western. If there is a need for someone to teach Indian history, well, it looks like we'll need an Indian person, or at least a person of Indian heritage to do that. Women's history? Better hire a woman for that. Interestingly, the only area where this does not occur is in the field of European or Western studies. In order to break down the distortions and perversions of Eurocentrism as quickly as possible, it is considered desirable to hire non-Westerners or at least persons of non-Western heritage to teach that subject since it will diversify the perspectives and root out all traces and remnants of Eurocentrism.

Here's the thing: I actually agree with the last point. Well, I agree with the idea, not the justification. I think the idea of having non-Western people immerse themselves in Western history, culture, politics—pretty much everything—and bringing those people into the educational system to provide diversely interesting viewpoints on various aspects of Western cultural history and cultural practices is a wonderful idea. What is wonderful about it is not that it breaks up the putative evil of Eurocentrism, but rather that it shows exactly what we need to do to make diversity work, something different from and something far beyond what we have now. To have non-Western peoples enter the world of knowledge regarding all things Western and incorporating those voices into what would then be a newly-enriched dialog on all things Western shows that cross-cultural learning is possible and desirable. One need not be a Westerner to master the elements of Western cultural knowledge any more than one needs to be Western to properly play the cello.

Here is where I explain why all of these recent trends in diversity education are a complete disaster. If it is good to diversify the narrative of all things Western by incorporating the voices of outsiders or "non-natives," then the same thing must be good for all similar narratives. And it is good for them because it helps to prevent the ossification of knowledge that all forms of *centrism* create. Yet that ossification is prevalent everywhere one looks in the strange world of diversity education. All one needs to do to see this is to walk down the halls of any university, or better still, go to their websites and look up the faculty. All of the departments that compose what is known as diversity education are usually the *least* diverse departments on any college campus. African-American departments will have African-American faculty, Latino studies will have Latino/a faculty, Native American studies will have Native American faculty, Women's studies will have women faculty, and so on. And with very few exceptions, students who major in those departments follow the same re-segregated patterns. Diversity education is thus the least diverse thing we have, even as it pats itself on the back for being so "radical" in how much diversity it promotes. Again, epic fail.

Diversity thought experiment #1
One of the ways that this re-segregation manifests itself on college campuses in the United States is through the presentation of what are called "cultural shows." In these cultural shows, different ethnic and racial groups create performances—often these are quite extravagant—in which students of specific ethnic or racial backgrounds showcase their culture. So for an Indian cultural show, for instance, there will always be a Bollywood routine and a cultural dance performance, and the Vietnamese cultural show will have Vietnamese students dressed in Vietnamese clothing, singing Vietnamese songs, doing Vietnamese dances, and so forth. There are many such shows on any given campus throughout the academic year. At UC Berkeley, at least, the audience will consist mostly of people from the ethnic group in question, along with students from that same group (to "show their support"), and a small handful of people from outside the community. All of these shows are held in the interest of "promoting diversity." The thing is, they don't actually promote diversity, at least in the sense of promoting understanding of other groups (which is how I have re-defined diversity). What they promote is ethnic solidarity within the same group, which is not diversity at all.

But now imagine a slightly different scenario. What if instead of self-promotion and self-centric solidarity, we restructured these types of events to promote diversity as cross-cultural understanding? What if we had, for instance, Indian cultural night, with the requirement that none of the participants could actually be Indian? Instead, students of non-Indian heritage—Vietnamese, European, Latino, and so on—would spend time learning about and mastering all of these performances, and would then perform them for the same audience as before. Imagine the same thing for the Vietnamese Cultural Night, then Latino Cultural Night, and so forth. Imagine a world where these shows actually diversified our thoughts and experiences of other cultures, imagine that they take a stand against the re-segregation created by diversity education. If you are having a hard time imagining it, or having a reluctance to think of it as a good idea, it only shows how far we are from attaining any type of meaningful and constructive diversity.

Diversity thought experiment #2
For this experiment, imagine you are walking around a college campus and you see flyers for a presentation on diversity education. It says that there will be speakers who will talk about different aspects of diversity on campus, and there will be introductory lectures from faculty from various departments that are part of the diversity education curriculum. You show up to the presentation, and the following occurs: the speaker for African-American issues is a white male, the speaker for Latino studies is a white male, the speaker for Native American studies is a white male, the speaker for Women's studies is a white male, and so on. Would you assume that something is wrong? Were you expecting or imagining a black speaker for African American studies, a Latino for Latino studies, a Native American for Native American studies, a woman for Women's studies? Is that what diversity looks like? It shouldn't. Think about it. Having a white male speaker for each of those different fields of knowledge is actually a radical act of diversity—it diversifies each of the fields by having an "outside" perspective that resists the tendency toward re-segregation through self-centrism. In other words, a feminist scholar lecturing on feminism in a way that promotes a feminist viewpoint is little different from a European imperialist lecturing on European imperialism in a way that promotes European imperialism. Whether Eurocentric or gynocentric—it's the same thing. And if you are thinking that there is no way a white male could ever learn those fields to the point of being accepted as a true expert, then I bet you must also think that Yo-Yo Ma is just awful at playing the cello.

Why the opposite of sensitivity can be diversity
I once gave a series of lectures in Hawai'i covering a variety of topics—surf culture and democracy, for instance, and the cultural history of the ukulele—and ended the lecture series with a cautionary lecture about how romanticizing Hawai'ian culture is as bad for Hawai'ian culture as it is for diversity. The lecture included a few examples of the less-than-romantic aspects from Hawai'ian history and culture. After the lecture, a woman came up to me, visibly irate, with the intent to lecture me on the virtues of Hawai'ian culture. She began to launch a diatribe about how "all you *haoles* from the mainland" come to Hawai'i and talk about Hawai'i without knowing and experiencing the "real Hawai'i" (a *haole* is someone in Hawai'i who is not a native Hawai'ian). I should also mention that this woman was not a native Hawai'ian but a transplant from Long Island. I tried to explain to her that I hadn't just arrived fresh off the boat but had spent much of my career immersed in this cultural environment. Why, I even tried to show her my Mahalo Rewards Card (*South Park* reference), but to no avail. Her advice to me was that I had to move to Hawai'i and live in the native environment long enough to "appreciate" the native culture, by which she meant that I would become sensitive and sympathetic to all things natively Hawai'ian to the point that I would no longer speak critically of it or think critically about it. I would just admire it. *All of it*. Even though this person was about as native to Hawai'i as a snake (culture note: Hawai'i has no snakes), the point she was making was not at all uncommon in these kinds of situations, and it is precisely why we need to mistrust the "authentic native" approach to diversity education. If we are so close to a culture that we feel only sympathy and sensitivity for it, we lose any chance to form a critical perspective. And if there is anything that diversity education should provide us with, it is a critical perspective—of ourselves and of others.

There are two fundamental problems that this unwarranted "feedback" to my lecture calls to our attention. The *first* is the way that diversity education has taken the form of cultural cheerleading: native experts are hired or appointed to show non-native outsiders how great their native culture is. The role of non-native outsiders is to accept this without question, which makes the process more like diversity indoctrination than diversity education. The *second* problem is that, given the strange and problematic state of diversity policy and practice in the present, native scholars are often seen by members of their own communities as representatives of their respective communities, a role which many of them accept and actively cultivate. The problem with this relationship is again, the absence of critical thinking. If a scholar or any educator is presenting information with the goal of gaining acceptance by and earning status within and obtaining credibility from the members of their community, then the whole enterprise is fatally compromised from the start. Sometimes it is actually better for this type of diversity education to hire someone who has no stake in the community or communities with which she or he interacts.

Keep in mind also that native voices aren't always good or even sensitive voices. I once had to sit through a rather painful joke told by a Bengali scholar (Bengali meaning from the Bengali-speaking area of eastern India) that described the "humorous" origin of the Tamil language (Tamil being a language of southern India and Sri Lanka). In this particular joke, the Bengali scholar described the sound of the Tamil language as the sound of the bubbles produced by God's flatulence in a bathtub. God had spent the day inventing the most beautiful language he could conceive—which not surprisingly was Bengali, since the joke was being told by a Bengali—and after spending so much effort crafting this beautiful language, he wanted to relax by taking a bath. When God had a fit of terrible flatulence, the Tamils, who were also waiting for God to give them a language and who were apparently not all that bright (certainly not as bright as the Bengalis), mistook the sound of the God's flatulence surfacing as bubbles in the water as their God-given language. So every time a Tamil person speaks his native tongue, it's like a fart from God bubbling up through the water. In other words, the Bengali language comes from the mouth of God, whereas Tamil comes out of the rectum. I should point out that all the Tamils in the room were greatly offended by this joke. What the anecdote reveals is just how misguided is the idea of finding an "Indian" to teach "Indian" things on the grounds that she or he authentically and automatically knows and understands everything about India. The Tamil language is just as foreign to a Bengali speaker as it is to someone like me, yet for some reason we assume that Indians somehow know all of India just by virtue of being Indian. And the reason we assume this is because diversity education encourages us to "find our own kind" and live in re-segregated enclaves.

On a follow up note, I will share a personal anecdote about my own experience in India, one that shows a moment of how diversity should actually work. First, for those who don't know this, let me explain that Hindi and Tamil are languages widely spoken in India, with Hindi spoken in the northern part of India and Tamil spoken in the southern part. I should also add that I have never in all my experiences of living in India or spending time with people from India encountered a native Hindi speaker who took the time to learn Tamil. They might exist, but I have never met one. Now, here is where I add that in my own studies, I have learnt both Hindi and Tamil. So one day, a few years back, when I was living in Madurai in the state of Tamil Nadu in southern India, a carpet-seller from Rajasthan, who was a native speaker of Hindi, came through my neighborhood trying to sell carpets. My next-door neighbor was interested in some of the carpets, but the carpet-seller spoke no Tamil and my next-door neighbor spoke no Hindi, so she quickly tried to think of someone who could help. Much to her amusement, and to the amusement of all my other neighbors who came out to watch, the only person in the area who could translate Tamil-to-Hindi and Hindi-to-Tamil was none other than yours truly, the White Man-in-residence who according to the urban legends of current diversity policy shouldn't be trusted to know anything about anything at all. My neighbor didn't end up buying a carpet—she thought his prices a bit too high—but it was a great moment where everyone learned a bit more about what cross-cultural understanding can do for the cultivation of meaningful diversity. It's also my way of saying that the current version of this thing called diversity education needs to pull its head out of its ethnocentric ass and start realizing that ethnocentrism, whether of the Euro variety or any other, is a disaster, and rewarding "native" sources of knowledge with their narcissistic expertise does nothing for the cause of diversity.

History never repeats except when it does which is almost always
One of the things that comes from the Foucault-laden approach to diversity education is an extreme sense of cultural relativism. The reasoning for this is relatively (pun actually intended) straightforward: any frame of reference one could imagine from which to judge other cultures would be considered a totalizing perspective. It would be one of those over-arching truths that according to Foucault means that someone is making a power grab to make us believe what we should not believe, and so must be rejected and resisted out of hand. The idea of extreme cultural relativism, where no one has the right to question or critique any cultural viewpoint other than their own, actually pairs well with a re-segregated society. We can all retreat into our smug little cultural enclaves where we question no one and no one questions us, and somehow—perhaps with a steady diet of meth-and-mezcal smoothies—we delude ourselves into thinking we have crafted diversity. Only a buffoon (or someone who actually lived on meth-and-mezcal smoothies) would see this as a good approach to diversity. For diversity to

work, there has to be a larger framework in which to embed the possibility of cross-cultural inquiry and cross-cultural dialog. The "trust no one" approach has to give way to a "learn to trust others" or "let others in" pattern of social interaction.

Few things shut down a dialog on diversity faster than someone invoking cultural relativism. It can be invoked in a number of ways, the most common and colloquial being the moment when someone says to an "outsider" that they "just don't get it" (something I have discussed in a number of scenarios throughout this book). To tell someone that they "just don't get it" really means something more like "you are challenging me in ways that make me uncomfortable and you are asking questions for which I have no compelling or logical answer so rather than answer I will just retreat to my own world and reject your questions and insights." It not only shuts down the dialog, it also prevents us from seeing patterns that would help us rethink the different ways that all of the elements of diversity fit together. For instance, if you have had the misfortune of suffering through any sort of program on diversity education, you will have no doubt come across a long-winded and derisory discussion of how those bad-ol'-Eurocentric imperialists of the nineteenth century arrogantly branded other cultures as over-sexed and erotically indulgent simply because they wore clothing (especially the women) that was considered indecently revealing by the prevailing Victorian standards of the time. I can't tell you how many mind-numbing lectures I have sat through in which the lecturer—usually in a voice loaded with dark sarcasm and that sort of superior laughter for which academics are famous—has commented at length on the how the sexually-repressed Victorian imperialists were really little more than well-traveled imperialist sex perverts. Sure, they denounced the cultures they saw as loose and sexually-depraved, but in reality they were actually envious of those cultures because they longed to do the same but could not do so because they were restrained by their own problematically hypocritical values. At this point, you might be thinking—*oh, haha, so true, so true.*

But now let me transpose the same situation into the present, and slightly alter the cultural framework. Picture the following situation, which is sadly not all that uncommon. Suppose now a Muslim family, living somewhere in the West, is dressed in clothing that follows what they interpret as Islamic standards of decency. The women in particular are wearing articles of clothing that cover most of their bodies, along with a veil or some other sort of religiously-appropriate head-covering—the specifics don't matter much for this hypothetical example. Now imagine as they walk down a sidewalk, a group of white Western women walk by—for this example let's assume it is summer—dressed in shorts and tank tops. The Muslim family watches them walk by, then talk among themselves about how Western women, by revealing so much in public, are just "whores." Now, let's apply the same "clever" analysis that I described above, only in this new transposed example, it would go something like this: "These Muslims are really just sexually-repressed people due to their problematically hypocritical values, and it is so clear that the Muslim men really want to be with the Western women and the Muslim women really just desire to be liberated like the Western women." My guess is at this point, if I were giving this as a lecture, you would never consider speaking up in the audience to say—*oh, haha, so true, so true*. In fact, even just reading what I described, you might have felt quite distressed and truly uncomfortable. Some of you might even have thought—*that's so Islamophobic*. In the context of diversity education, we as an audience are "strongly urged" to interpret the example through the eyes of the Muslim family, to understand their values and try to make sense of why they would feel that way about Western women. That, we would be told, is the type of "cultural sensitivity" that diversity education should inculcate.[26]

---

26 Though my example is hypothetical, there are real-world examples of this, including situations where immigrant families have killed their own family

And I would be fine with that, as long as it were consistently applied. Don't give me a lecture about how those stupid and hypocritical Westerners totally judged foreign cultures by stupidly inserting their own values into a foreign environment, and then tell me I need to understand and to a certain extent condone the reaction of the Muslim family by understanding their values in a "proper" context. The reactions of the nineteenth-century European imperialists, whose dress codes ironically resembled those of many contemporary Muslim societies, also make perfect sense if we understand their values in a "proper" context. Should we therefore be more tolerant toward European imperialism? Or perhaps we should start condemning those scholars who criticize Eurocentrism as "Europhobic." If we expected Europeans who went to other cultures to blend into those cultures and appreciate and adopt the values of their host societies, shouldn't we also expect that sort of assimilation from all immigrant cultures in the West in the present? In any case, if diversity education is going to start doing something useful, it is going to have iron out these incredibly naïve inconsistencies in its many narratives.

Chronological relativism
There are those who would point out the shift in time between these two examples—one from the nineteenth century and one from the present—but that doesn't resolve the tension between the disparate treatment of similar examples as much as it raises a whole new issue that so far no one has really cared or dared to raise in all of this. Even more important than addressing cultural relativism is the importance of addressing what I would call

---

members for wanting to assimilate. See, for example, Jody K. Biehl, "The Death of a Muslim Woman: "The Whore Lived Like a German"," *Der Spiegel Online* (March 2, 2005) at http://www.spiegel.de/international/the-death-of-a-muslim-woman-the-whore-lived-like-a-german-a-344374.html

chronological relativism. Just as cultural relativism tells us that we cannot judge other cultures by the values of our own, chronological relativism cautions us not to judge the actions of the past by the values of the present. We condemn the "racism" of European empires, but largely from a standpoint of human rights values of the present that cannot be applied to the past. In the nineteenth century, neither racism nor imperialism were seen as wrong or even illegal, and so demanding justice in the present for what was done in the past—especially when as we have seen in earlier chapters there were so many other empires for which the issue of justice has been ignored—is a very tricky issue to wade into. It is especially difficult to avoid the issue of chronological relativism when it is unevenly applied, as with the two examples just discussed about Eurocentric perceptions of the past and Islamocentric perspectives of the present.

I have sat through lectures and heard presentations about how it is wrong to condemn the Mayans (among others) for their practice of human sacrifice because it made sense to them given their values *at that time.* To judge them from the present, or to judge them as early Spanish explorers did, is simply wrong. Fine. But if that is true, it becomes impossible to condemn, for instance, slavery in the United States, since in those areas where it was practiced it was not illegal at the time and those who engaged in the practice certainly thought it "made sense" and was justified by their values at the time. (Note that I am *not* saying slavery was therefore acceptable, but simply pointing out what happens to our understanding of history if we introduce chronological relativism.) All of these forms of relativism need to be dealt with in a constructive way, largely because of the way they jeopardize the possibility of meaningful dialog in the present. We are haplessly inconsistent in the way we look at the differences between cultures in the present, just as we are haplessly inconsistent in how we look at those differences in the past. Justice requires consistency, so if we are hoping to link justice with diversity, then clearly, something better needs to be done.

Thinking differently about diversity education
As I've mentioned previously, one of the more troubling questions I get, pretty much everywhere I go when I give lectures, are questions that go something like this: How did you get interested in Asia? How did you decide to study India? These questions always come from students whose heritage is rooted in those regions, and what I find disturbing about these questions is the subtext behind them. What they are really asking is this: I am of Indian heritage so of course I would study India, but why would you? Or, I am of Japanese heritage so of course I would study Japanese things, but why you? This is yet another snapshot that shows everything that is so wrong with diversity education: it encourages everyone to go in search of their own culture, their own community, and yet we still seem puzzled as to why we do not understand each other better across our cultural divides. The better and more important question that diversity education should ask of all of those who have queried my choices is this: why did you let your race or culture determine your academic interests? Why are you so interested only in yourself? Why do you complain that other people do not understand your culture when your own choice reflects a complete lack of interest in understanding theirs? If you want to learn about yourself and develop a deep-seated sense of narcissism about your own culture or identity-group, then you should do so on your own time. On the clock of diversity time, in the classroom of diversity education, the task at hand is to learn to understand others. Check your selves at the door.

One of the cinematic gems to come out of the East Bay (as in, the East Bay of the San Francisco Bay Area) is a little film called *East Side Sushi* (2014), directed by Anthony Lucero. Set mostly in Oakland, the film follows the story of a Latina chef with aspirations to become a master sushi chef. She works in a Japanese restaurant, but quickly bumps up against a roadblock to her aspirations. It isn't the white man, as diversity always wants us to believe, but rather Japanese men, who quickly inform Juana (the character's name) that to be a master sushi chef a person must be (1) Japanese and (2) male. Juana quickly sets out to prove them wrong, puzzling her father who can't understand why she isn't sticking with Latin cuisine. I won't give away the ending, but what I like about the movie is that it shows a glimpse of the kind of diversity we should be pursuing. The haters who keep puking out diatribes against cultural appropriation should especially watch this film, as it shows how diversity simply cannot succeed without cultural appropriation. Juana isn't betraying Latina culture, and she isn't stealing Japanese culture either. She's charting her own, empowering pathway to a better diversity for all of us.

Who has the right to learn and acquire knowledge about other cultures and other identities? Who has the right to convey that information to others? Who has the right to scrutinize and think critically about the information they gain? The answer to these questions is the same answer as the one given to the question of who has the right to pick up the cello and learn to play: *anyone*. The trend we have followed for the past few years to put "native experts" in place, in the name of diversity education, has been a gruesome mistake that will probably take a whole other generation to undo. It has created a form of self-made ethnic profiling in which distorted and self-centric narratives are fed uncritically and selectively to a learning public that is asked to accept things without question (or else risk being seen as "culturally insensitive"). We should stop expecting the Chinese chef at the Chinese restaurant, or the Filipino professor of Filipino history, and instead look for the true innovators of diversity—those that break away from their cultural constraints and seek out new pathways to cross-cultural understanding. If the criticism against Eurocentrism is valid for one reason, it is valid for the way it shows that all self-centric modes of understanding share the same biases, and these biases do far more harm to the possibility of diversity than good. We've already seen what happens when people view the world through their own narcissistic lens, and it doesn't end well. What we should expect and demand from diversity education is not a story about "my people" and about ourselves, nor one that requires us to admire others without question. What we need is a new approach to diversity education that allows us to see ourselves among others, a perspective that is both reflective mirror and transparent window. If I could build a school to make that happen, I'd engrave this on the front gate: *Only a moron complains about the food without ever learning to cook.*

CHAPTER 3

WE ARE ALL IMPERIALISTS NOW

Diversity will require nothing less than the complete rewriting of human history. There, I said it. If the previous chapter focused on the need to tell our histories with equal candor, the good along with the bad, then this chapter focuses on how our fatally-flawed perspective of one specific historical moment has generated so much bitterness, so much vindictiveness, so much truculent drama, so much accusatory hostility, and so much incessantly infantile prattle, that diversity has almost become well-nigh impossible. That historical moment, really more of a complex historical phenomenon, can be summarized in one word: *imperialism* (or its not quite synonymous counterpart, colonialism). Though it may not appear that way on the surface, so much of diversity policy, even or perhaps especially in America, is an attempt to respond to and to redress nearly every aspect of this one historical moment. Diversity thus becomes seen as a form of restorative justice for a perceived historical wrong, one that is unyielding in its complexity and hence susceptible to convenient and manipulative oversimplification.

The idea of rendering justice for historical phenomena is even on the best of days fraught with nearly insurmountable problems, and when our perceptions of what happened in the past are so skewed and incomplete and our chronological lens so myopic and opaque, then any hope of meaningful and substantive justice becomes lost, even before we begin. In its place, we are left only with a profound sense of mistrust and betrayal and a misplaced wistfulness for things that we think might have been but in reality never were and never will be. Any platform of diversity that leaves this crucial historical moment unexamined will be a diversity that is more myth than substance, and a grave penchant for myth is the hubris of diversity. What we need right now is not myth but grit—the courage to face the past, the courage to face ourselves, and the courage to change what needs to be changed, which is pretty much everything.

Nostalgia and chronological narcissism
As yet another example of how perceptions of what happened long ago directly impact our lives in the present, consider the case of Mohamed Atta. Mohamed Atta was one of the murderers who participated in the hijackings and the other heinous acts of terrorism that killed so many innocent people and harmed so many lives on September 11, 2001. It was clear that Atta was full of hate, but what precisely made him so full of hate? There are those who mumble things about "US foreign policy" and "hegemony" and other incessantly insipid blah blah blah forms of commentary, but those sorts of people are looking only at secondary levels of causality and making only surface connections that are tenuous at best. No, what Atta hated more than anything was the idea that something "foreign" had infiltrated and sullied what he had come to believe should be the purest bastion of identity in his own little self-appointed bailiwick: the Islamic world. For Atta, who studied urban planning as a graduate student, utopia was simple: there should be no trace of Western or foreign culture in the heart of an Islamic landscape. Everything should be Islamic and nothing should be foreign. For mile after mile after mile, in other words, there should be no diversity whatsoever. What Atta hated more than anything was diversity.

Atta wrote a master's thesis in the field of urban planning while he was a student at the Hamburg Institute of Technology in Germany—yes, that's right, at a Western university. The subject of his thesis was the Syrian city of Aleppo, more specifically the older part of Aleppo, and the fundamental tenor of the thesis was that Aleppo had been a "traditional" Islamic city until it was ruined by the introduction of Western ideas about urban planning. Streets had been straightened, high-rises and skyscrapers had been introduced (these he hated more than anything), highways had been built to facilitate urban interaction from one part of the city to another, shopping centers had been redesigned to facilitate commerce—in essence, elements of modern efficiency, so much the rage in dominant schools of modernist urban planning, had been introduced and implemented in Aleppo. What Atta's thesis does is outline a plan to erase all of these foreign layers of Aleppo and to restore the city to what it had been in the past, before these foreign things had arrived. He wanted to reintroduce the crooked streets, the traditional markets, and he wanted to dismantle and level all the high-rise buildings, all so that Aleppo could once again become a city of traditional Islamic people living in a traditional Islamic environment living traditional Islamic lives. Atta was obsessed with the idea that Aleppo should have been something else and *would* have been something else if only the foreign West had not intervened. He was also obsessed with the idea of restoring Aleppo to its original essence. In other words, Atta wanted to reverse history, something that, as we shall see, is completely and utterly impossible.

The leap from architecture and urban planning to religious-based terrorism might seem an implausible one, but Atta's fundamental world-view on urban planning elided quite effortlessly with the hopelessly stunted world-view of the movement he ultimately joined—al-Qaeda. I know there are those who see al-Qaeda as a movement inspired by justice and resistance by the oppressed against their Western oppressors, but those people need to move beyond the superficial rhetoric and go straight to the foundational aspects of al-Qaeda's ideology. Part of al-Qaeda's ideology does indeed call for the killing of Americans and Westerners in general, based on their militant opposition to the idea of Western powers meddling in the Islamic world. But part of it is also inspired by the misguided belief of Atta and others like him that history can be cleansed and corrected by reversing its path.

Al-Qaeda is not opposed only to what is foreign and un-Islamic. They are also opposed to other Muslims who do not adhere to their interpretation of what Islam is and how it should be practiced. Shia Muslims, liberal Muslims, Muslims who engage in *ijtihad* (an Arabic world referring to the effort to use one's own mind and the principles of Islam to resolve matters of personal and religious difficulty)—all of these are targeted as threats to the presumed purity of al-Qaeda's world-view. Like many religiously-inspired militant groups, al-Qaeda is so convinced that its world-view is the only true and acceptable world-view for humanity that its struggle cannot end until the ultimate endpoint is achieved: the whole world is dominated by Islam, and not just by Islam, but by the type of Islam that al-Qaeda promotes. One world, one religion, one version of that religion, one type of thought, one way of life. Nothing would be foreign to anyone, because the whole world would be the same. In other words, in the view of al-Qaeda, when there is no diversity left, utopia begins.

This is not the place to go into the flaws of al-Qaeda's ideology—other scholars, Islamic and otherwise, have already done so at length. What I am interested in here is the way that al-Qaeda's vision of history, like Mohamed Atta's, is based upon two central beliefs: (1) that a lack of diversity is a positive and comforting thing, and (2) that history somehow went "off course" and can and should be corrected. As with so many other things that relate to diversity as it currently exists, there is no shortage of hypocrisy here: note for instance how Atta personally and al-Qaeda generally are outraged by the introduction of what is non-Islamic into what is Islamic, but have no problem with and indeed actively promote introducing what is Islamic into what is non-Islamic. That is, they denounce the infidel presence in Islamic lands, but gladly promote an Islamic presence in non-Islamic lands. *Please do not do to me what I insist on doing to you*—that's not a plan for utopia, that's a plan for hypocrisy.

Similarly, the fundamental flaw in Atta's thinking was that Aleppo would have been real and organic and authentic without the foreign elements it allegedly contained. Erase the agglutination of foreign filth built up on layers of filched history, the argument goes, and the residue that remains will be only the purest of culture, the authenticity of which is directly predicated on its lack of diversity. But here is the central problem: what Atta thought was the one and true traditional Aleppo was in fact created through the conquest and transformation of the city during periods of Islamic rule. Atta was lamenting the introduction of the foreign into a city whose foundation was itself created earlier by the introduction of the foreign. Every layer of Aleppo, from first to last, is equally foreign.

Mohamed Atta may have joined forces with a radical and militant group of terrorists, but the ideas he espoused about urban planning and culture are far more common than one might think. Keep in mind that the leap to terrorism is an extraordinary one, and therefore we cannot make the mistake of assuming that those who think about cities or history in ways similar to Mohamed Atta are also likely to engage in terrorism. What we can conclude, however, is that those who espouse similar modes of thinking are also those who do the greatest amount of damage to the promise and potential of diversity. What I refer to here are those who have the desire to turn back the clock of time—to reverse historical progression—to a point where one's own identity group is returned to a presumed pristine state, to a point where things were as they should have been, to a point where identity was simple and homogeneous. Keep in mind that these historically misplaced utopias are complete nonsense, but their allure is for many simply too powerful to resist. Narcissism is never too far away from efforts to forge a sense of group-based identity out of innate characteristics (such as ethnicity), but here we add a temporal element where an impossible wish for purity in the present becomes a realizable dream when it is projected into the past. And after it is viewed in all its myopic splendor as a misremembered but reinvented past, it becomes a blueprint for a possible future. Marx once famously suggested that religion was the opiate of the masses, by which he meant that religion made it possible to anaesthetize the oppressed masses from the reality of their oppression. When it comes to diversity, history itself is the opiate of the identity-obsessed masses.

This opiate-induced historical hallucination takes on any one of a number of forms—an Africa where only Africans ruled in benevolent kingdoms, a Chicano-only kingdom known as Aztlán, an India that was only Hindu, an America of only white people with even whiter picket fences, or an Aleppo devoid of skyscrapers and anything else deemed un-Islamic—but they all are just variants of the same siren song of race-pride and identity-based triumphalism, with a war-drum backbeat beckoning to those predisposed to militancy, should they be among us. Indeed, as a most extreme example, the entire project of the Islamic State has been to reverse the shifting sands of time—to *restore* the Caliphate (lost at the hands of foreigners), to *recreate* the purity of the earliest Islamic community (before diversity of belief set in), and so on. There is something inexplicably seductive about going back to a point in time when things seemed so pure and simple, and strangely, so many of these imagined moments—and do be sure that all of these moments exist only in the imagination—involve a complete and utter lack of diversity. Paradise was lost when foreigners arrived and took our purity away. So much diversity babble is a misguided lamentation for the loss of something that had never been gained in the first place. This seductive lamentation for an imagined past that was lost, for a time when identity was perfect, is something I call *chronological narcissism*.

Falling in love with the person I never was
There are many peculiar things about this chronological narcissism, but perhaps what is most peculiar about it is how so much of it has clustered around one moment in history where supposedly everything went "wrong." As I have already hinted, this one moment in history, a moment whose historical gravity is allegedly so strong that it occludes and distorts all other historical moments, is the moment of *imperialism*. Mohamed Atta hated what Aleppo had become, and he traced his hatred back in time only to the moment when Europeans arrived, only to the moment when the "foreign" arrived in white, European form. If only that moment could be expunged, extirpated, erased, eviscerated—Aleppo would return to its once-upon-a-time true essence. It would be authentic again. What is equally peculiar, and perhaps more disturbing, is how the architects of these imagined historical moments—those whose craft it is to build historical narratives, that is, historians—are inescapably and inexcusably complicit in the perpetuation of this historical farce. Historians and other so-called thinkers perpetuate this myth that imperialism is the moment in time when wholesome tradition was ruptured around the world and morally-bankrupted Western modernity was forced down the gullet of the world to create the fetid *foie gras* of Eurocentric civilization, which was then replicated infinitely in any and every direction one cared to look.

Scholars such as Paul Rabinow have written for instance of how European urban planners—in Rabinow's case he focused on French urban planners—spoiled so many cities in the Francophone reaches of empire by turning them into laboratories of colonial control through the fulcrum of urban planning. In various outposts of empire, urban designs were transposed onto existing cities, whose forms were accepted as organic and tangibly authentic by Rabinow, and in this transposition, urban architecture was made not just to represent colonial power but also to distort the very texture of the city so that it served the interests of empire. Urban design became a tool of imperial power. Authentic traditional structures of the colonized were dismantled and looted and in their place an artificially foreign urban apparatus was constructed to facilitate the infusion of (French, in this case) colonial values onto colonized subjects and to obfuscate anything incompatible with the needs and momentum of colonial rule.

Mohamed Atta was inebriated with these ideas: underneath the taint of foreign and European structures was the pure, traditional, and authentic Aleppo.[27] But in reality, what Atta and Rabinow and so many others have missed, wittingly or unwittingly, is that the old Aleppo underneath was itself already a monument of control and power. The great revelation of history in this context is that the French imperialists had done nothing new. They had introduced an artificial layer onto a city already composed of so many other artificial layers. They substituted one form of urban-induced order for another, one form of power for another. The French were not the first nor will they be the last to restructure Aleppo. *All cities are monuments to one form of power or another.* It is not by accident that Atta spoke in his dissertation about recreating "traditional" neighborhoods to keep women hidden away and to prevent them from having any thoughts of emancipation. Atta's traditional design

---

27 For more on Atta's dissertation and his world-view, see Daniel Brook, "The Architect of 9/11," *Slate* (September 8, 2009) at http://www.slate.com/articles/news_and_politics/dispatches/features/2009/the_architect_of_911/what_can_we_learn_about_mohamed_atta_from_his_work_as_a_student_of_urban_planning.html

wanted to prevent one form of emancipation, and French colonial design wanted to prevent another. The more Aleppo changes, the more it stays the same.

In other words, colonial modernity and foreign ideas did not ruin Atta's precious Aleppo any more than they ruined any other city, unless we concede that all cities are ruined from their inception. An ideal Islamic city and an ideal colonial city are conceptual twins separated at birth: put them together side by side, and you can't help but see the similarities. And this applies to any planned city, not merely Islamic or colonial, but any planned environment. Planning and power are inseparable. (They are also insufferable, nearly all of the time, but that is a tangent that will have to wait.) Modernist Aleppo and traditional Aleppo are not two discrete or opposite entities: neither is more "real" than the other and neither is the city that "should have been." Yet we persist in believing, and many so-called scholars encourage us to believe, that what was there before the West arrived was somehow real and authentic, and then this was destroyed or lost at the historical moment when the foreigners arrived. In many ways, Edward Said's classic work *Orientalism*, discussed in a previous chapter, is a part of this trend. This is one of the biggest conceptual flaws we have in the entire story of human history. It perpetuates the destructive fictions of chronological narcissism, and these fictions may have undermined the possibility of a vibrant intercultural society and a well-crafted sense of diversity in the present.

America and so many other parts of the world have been torn apart and so many lives rent asunder by the misguided desire to "set history right," to go back in time to the moment before foreigners arrived to recapture the putative utopia of social homogeneity. This notion was actually a central motivating factor in the ideology of the Khmer Rouge, the group that carried out the Cambodian genocide that occurred between April 1975 and January 1979 (and discussed in the previous chapter). If Cambodia could be cleansed of everything that was foreign—in their mindset, akin to Atta, this included cities themselves, which were brutally emptied of their inhabitants shortly after the Khmer Rouge came to power—it would return to and recapture its former glory. Ironically that former glory included an ethnic Khmer *empire,* and so as with Atta, there is a tremendous dose of hypocrisy here. The idea was not to liberate the authentic and real structures from the inauthentic and foreign colonial structures, but rather to change one structure of colonial power for another. Anti-imperialists and imperialists seem secretly to hold each other in high regard, it seems, historical rhetoric to the contrary.

While I am on the point, I may as well bring up another facet of this whole intellectual burlesque act, one that will presage what is soon to follow in this discussion. I find it interesting and not a little amusing that the very same scholars who champion this idea that the impetus of colonial modernity undermined and destroyed traditional life in colonial metropoles one after another like a freight-train of foreign fiendishness are also the first to scoff at the idea that the arrival of immigrants and foreigners in the West may have somehow undermine American or European traditions. When Westerners go to other countries, it seems—and note again how in this scenario a Westerner is always assumed to be white—the traditions of those countries are lost, but when those in other countries come to the West, the traditions of the West are enriched through diversity. There is a strange conservatism at work here. Somehow, the rest of the world should stay as it is, indeed should be preserved and protected *from* the West, but *in* the West, we should accept and promote change through diversity. We are revolutionary for ourselves and yet reactionary for others, for the same reason in both cases. Confused? As I said, this business of purifying history is an impossible dream. Diversity cannot restore the past, and for that matter, nothing can change the past. History never had a direction and time does not have a motive. Aleppo was not changed from what it should have been. It simply became something else, as it had so many times before. History does not change its direction; the change of direction *is* history.

In case I have overemphasized the role of urban planning, I should point out that this impulsive proclivity to bring history again and again back to this one moment in time—when imperialism arrived—extends into every single facet of the past one can imagine. I once attended a panel discussion on imperialism where the topic at hand was the idea of the "civilizing mission"— the belief by Europeans that European imperialism had a duty to bring the benefits of advanced civilization (which Europe thought it had achieved) to the rest of the world. Suddenly a woman in the audience, a woman from India, stood up and informed everyone in attendance that India already had an advanced civilization at a time when Europeans were still "living in caves." This was followed by whoops of delight and spontaneous applause by those in the audience and those on the panel. As for me, I was puzzled by these theatrics. I'm not sure how reversing the premise takes us anywhere other than to the same cerebral cesspool, albeit from a different direction. If it is evidence of arrogance for Europeans to think they had a more advanced civilization than others, then for Indians to think the same way is just as arrogant. Nor do I understand this desire to turn history into a race. Does it really matter who had "lots" of civilization or when they might have had it? Is there really a discussion somewhere in the world that goes something like this?

Non-Indian: *I read a report recently that said that currently there are more people living below the poverty line in India than there are in all of Africa.*

Indian: *You must remember that India had lots of civilization when Europeans were still living in caves.*

Non-Indian: *I see. Because history is apparently some sort of race and because India felt it was in the lead many centuries ago, I must be mistaken in my views of the present so please accept my apologies.*[28]

We could talk incessantly about how this line of reasoning is haplessly pathetic—one is reminded of the Bruce Springsteen song "Glory Days"—but the wrench in the works of lucidity brings us back to this thing with history and imperialism. The whole point of the comment at the panel discussion, the unspoken longer narrative of which it is a part, is that India's civilization would have continued to be far ahead of Europe, and India would today be a great superpower, if imperialism hadn't "changed history" and stolen India's glory away. Never mind that the logic here simply replicates (by inversion) the imperialist argument: that advanced civilization gives one rights and privileges over others. The logic behind all of this is that when imperialism happened, the world, or in this case India, went "off course." (Again, history cannot go "off course.") And since imperialism also brought things like racism, and since racism has something to do with diversity, somehow diversity is at least in part devised as a way to "set history right" again by reversing the damage done by imperialism. Diversity restores the authentic identities lost by the intrusion of imperialism into foreign lands. Something is very strange about the lamentation of the West into the non-West but the championing of the non-West into the West. We end up with all sorts of inexplicable and irreconcilable conclusions: why is Christianity a "foreign" religion in India but Buddhism is a "native" religion in Japan? We need more than a warts-and-all telling of historical narratives to move us forward.

---

28 The claim, incidentally, is true. See Jason Burke, "More of world's poor live in India than in all sub-Saharan Africa, says study," *The Guardian* (July 13, 2010) at http://www.theguardian.com/world/2010/jul/14/poverty-india-africa-oxford

We need a completely new understanding of history itself to make diversity work. Actually, we need it to make humanity work, but we can start with diversity, for now.

Diversifying imperialism
When I asked in an earlier discussion about what image people thought of when they thought of the "dumb American," I pointed out that in moments when negative things are discussed, advocates of diversity go silent. No one wants to hear that idiocy is multicultural and diverse. In the present discussion on the power of history to craft and distort our entire approach to diversity, I will make the same argument with a slightly different perspective. For this approach, consider the following question: when you see the word imperialism or colonialism, without any sort of qualifying adjective, what historical phenomenon does your mind conjure? If you answered European imperialism, then you are safely in line with pretty much everyone else. The same is true of other related words: when someone describes her- or himself as "post-colonial" (more on which shortly), we know the historical referent is European imperialism and colonialism. We don't even ask for more information. We simply assume.

This assumption, however, is a dangerous one, one that burdens the entire project of diversity with a continuous and contradictory "suspension of belief" approach whereby we are required to learn more and more about marginalized identity-groups but are also required to learn only the positive things that those groups want us to know. In other words, the history of the world as told by the dominant group must be resisted because it conveniently serves the needs of the dominant group by censoring out inconvenient facts. But the real problem here is not that history was written by the dominant group. *The problem is the censorship.* Any censorship. *All* censorship. Too many advocates of diversity have put the emphasis on the former while bypassing the latter. That is, they have advocated that the dominant group is the problem and so non-dominant groups by default must be non-problems; if dominant groups are bad, then non-dominant groups must be good. History is then crafted around those assumptions, so that history can be put in the service of diversity to create a history that represents all groups equally. But if history is going to represent all groups equally, we have to remove the blinders of censorship to get there, because if blinders are given only to one group and not to others, this precludes the premise of equality in history. Once we remove these blinders, two things will happen: (1) history will get equally ugly for all of us, and (2) a new diversity, one that is actually sustainable and attainable for all, will finally become possible.

Let's return to the point about how imperialism and colonialism, when used as is, refer to this one moment in time, the time when Europeans (only some of them, actually) went out to conquer the world. I think it is fair to say that the general assumption about this moment in time is that it is considered the grand moment when "history changed" and the world that should have been became something it was never supposed to be (and to belabor the point again, history cannot change—the change itself *is* history). So much of our current approach to diversity is anchored in this one historical moment. Talk of restorative justice, demands for reparations, efforts to reclaim authentic identities, plans to remove skyscrapers from Aleppo, and so many other things, are all connected to the obsession with reversing the damage done by European imperialism. Now, I am certainly not going to argue that European imperialism was not a destructive force, and I am even going to agree with the premise that everywhere it went, it certainly created perturbations and problems. What I *am* going to argue, however, is that this moment of history, this moment of imperialism that forms the centerpiece of so much discussion about identity-formation, human rights, global justice, and so on—*this historical moment was nothing new and nothing special.* If we open up our historical inquiry equally wide, we will see that all of us are imperialists in one form or other. Yes, as I have said many times before, equality and diversity come in negative flavors as well.

New wine in very old bottles
I am always dismayed and frequently bored by the mind-eroding introduction I frequently hear in any discussion of identity-formation that includes a discussion of history. That introduction goes something like this: "if you want to know where the problems started, we have to go back to the arrival of the colonizer (or "white man", etc.)…" Apparently, and amazingly, before that moment, there were no problems in the world: children smiled, parents loved children, birds sang, everyone hugged trees and the trees hugged back. This image is as common in colloquial discourse as it is in intellectual discourse—recall the "can't we just blame imperialism?" comment from the previous chapter.

But let's have some fun and push beyond the limits of this incredulously naïve approach to world history and start somewhere a bit more random. Ancient Egypt, you say? Excellent choice. Much of what we know about ancient Egypt as we like to remember it—that is, in its most advanced and sophisticated stages of civilization (note again how advanced civilization becomes a marker of identity, no matter where we find it)—starts to emerge during what is referred to as the Naqaba III period (3200-3000 BCE). One of the most important reasons for the expansion in complexity of ancient Egyptian society and polity at this time was the rapidly increasing circulation of wealth through expanding networks of regional trade. One central truism in history is that where you find money you will find other people who want that money, and ancient Egypt is no exception to that rule. Naqaba III culture emerged out of the interaction and contestation between southerners and northerners (refrain from thinking of them all as "Egyptians" for the moment since the state of Egypt did not exist until many centuries later). Southerners were drawn north by the expansion in trade, literally to cash in on the action, and the traders who arrived were then followed by colonizers. Here is how one scholar of the period describes what happened: "A motivating factor for the expansion of the Naqaba culture into northern Egypt might have been the desire to gain direct control over the lucrative trade with other regions in the eastern Mediterranean, which had developed earlier in the fourth millennium BC."[29] No doubt this observation seems somewhat predictable, and no doubt no one is really worked up about how the southerners expanded into the north to try to gain control of the regional trade and the wealth it generated. It is just part of the landscape, part of the intrigue and allure of the history of ancient Egypt.

But now, just for a bit of mischief, let me offer the exact same sentence, only this time I will make a few key substitutions, and then watch how quickly everything seems to change. Here is the reworded sentence (with substitutions in italics): "A motivating factor for the expansion of *the British* into *India* might have been the desire to gain direct control over the lucrative trade with other regions *in South Asia*, which had developed earlier in the *eighteenth century*." Does this reworded sentence generate an entirely different sentiment? Do you feel a sense of outrage about how the knavish British went to a different place to gain control of the wealth being generated there? I mean, who did the British think they were, going to India like that? I'll tell you who the British were: *they were everyone else in human history*. They did what so many other groups of people had done before. The spoiler alert of world history is that European imperialism was nothing new, a sequel to a film already made one too many times and already awful the first time it was made (think *Weekend at Bernie's* remade as *Twilight*).

---

29 Kathryn A. Bard, "The Emergence of the Egyptian State," *Oxford History of Ancient Egypt* (Oxford), 62

But wait, you might say. The British were very different because they brought with them a cultural arrogance and an unjust hierarchy between colonizer and colonized that no one else had ever done before. Lines were crossed, and things were done that should never have been done. British imperialism was unique and not like anything else. Really? Here are a few more details about the history of ancient Egypt as it was built up on the filched trade of the Mediterranean region. As a result of the successful wresting of control of regional trade, conquest soon followed, as did the flourishing of a new, hierarchical society (the haves and the have-nots existed here, too, as they do in all forms of imperialism). Why, there was even art: "The king and his officials are shown in the special dress of their offices, while their conquered enemies wear next to nothing."[30] Indeed, conquering and humiliating others was even funny: "The king is frequently depicted trampling on his enemies, in visual puns." If you are struggling to find ways to create distance between this information about ancient Egypt and British imperialism, or if your brain is having a hard time processing this information (and trying hard to resist seeing the self-evident parallels), then you are experiencing the first hint that everything we think we know about world history, and by association, everything we think we can expect from diversity in the present, is based on a complete misreading of human history.

The short and bitter truth is that imperialism is as ubiquitous in the history of humanity as is flatulence, and anyone who wants to argue that one culture's version is far more severe or different from another's is going to be wrong on both counts. Imperialism has created countless chapters of misery, death, destruction, and devastation, but it has done so in every single occurrence where it has reared its ugly and power-hungry head. The imperialism of Europe was only one variety among many, a variation on a theme,

---

30 *Ibid.*, 81 (for this and following quote)

and to pin the entire world's injustices on that particular moment can only be done with the kind of distortive power that is associated with black holes, fascism, or *Night Train* (as in the wine and *not* the amplifier, though arguably both are associated with a unique type of distortion). *What is remarkable about European imperialism is how unexceptional it is.* Many if not most of the peoples who have considered themselves "colonized" victims of imperialists were at one time or other themselves imperialists, or at least aspired to be. Imperialism is wrong since it thrives on the suppression and exploitation of others, and the key thing to remember here is that if it is wrong at one point in history, it is wrong at *all* points in history.

Making China great again
Think, for instance, of this anomaly: if imperialism is such an awful thing, why then do we gloss over the label "Imperial China" as if somehow the imperial part is not linked to imperialism? The current boundaries of China, for instance, are based on the expanded borders of China's historical imperialist expansion. Many scholars lament at how the world map was drawn up according to imperialism—so-called "artificial" borders created by European imperialism—but those borders are no more artificial than the borders of present-day China. (This isn't to single-out China—there are very few borders anywhere on earth that aren't in some way artificial.) For some, and as discussed earlier, the current rise of China is often viewed, even by the Chinese government, as an appropriate return for an empire that was once the "central kingdom" (the Mandarin name for China, *zhongguó*, means exactly that), until of course the nineteenth century came along and European empires overshadowed China's power. But look closely at that moment: the nineteenth century, the so-called century of shame in Chinese history, is little more than a moment when one set of imperialists undermined the plans of another. When China was an empire in

the making, it expanded from a small heartland and one at a time violently conquered other peoples who clearly did not want to be a part of the Chinese empire (and many of those peoples still don't want to be a part of China today). Yet the bloody expansion of "Imperial China" is seen as a good thing, and many Chinese people, whether in China or elsewhere, look at the label with pride, evoking a long-lost sort of glory. Why is the imperialism of others, though just as destructive and just as violent as the European variety—why are these other imperialisms looked on as great accomplishments, moments of pride and celebration? It is a travesty of common sense, human dignity, and basic justice to view history this way.

At the risk of repeating myself, let's revisit my previous discussion of one of the so-called "great monuments" built by the Chinese empire as a testament to the desire to prevent others from threatening their power: the Great Wall. If you travel to China, there are countless tours available to showcase this marvel to tourists, where it is shown with pride as an amazing architectural achievement and evidence of China's advanced civilization. Yet what is the Great Wall other than a giant wall to keep foreigners and other "barbarians" out of China's imperialist boundaries? In its intent, it is little different from the wall built by Israel to prevent Palestinians from entering the country. Indeed, it is little different from Donald Trump's plan to build a wall between Mexico and the United States. Yet Israel's wall and Trump's (planned) wall are universally condemned as racist and inhumane, while China's wall is seen as "Great" and a marvel of the world. Would anyone be willing to accept a new cultural history of the world that talks of the Great Wall of Israel or the Great Wall of Trump in glowing terms? Probably not—big walls usually tell of big problems and ugly beliefs, no matter where they are or when they were built.

China's Not-So-Great Wall is not that surprising of a monument, given the long history ethnic Han chauvinism in China's history (and in present-day China as well). (For those unfamiliar with Chinese society and politics, the dominant ethnic group in China is the ethnic Han, and even back in the empire-building days of China, the ethnic Han assumed themselves to be superior to all other groups...again, sound familiar?) During the Qing dynasty period (1644-1911), for instance, when the group that ruled China came from the minority ethnic Manchu community, many ethnic Han Chinese bristled at the idea that a minority could possibly rule the great empire of China. "Secret societies" were formed and rebellions were launched by ethnic Han groups to put rulers from the dominant ethnic group back on the imperial throne. Anti-foreignism is a recurrent theme in modern Chinese history, and though many a Chinese history textbook celebrates the anti-foreignism of the Boxer Rebellion (the anti-foreignism against "the Imperialists," that is, the Europeans in China), when that same anti-foreignism is directed against members of the dominant ethnic Han group, the history textbooks go silent. Whether in Inner Mongolia or in Tibet or in Xinjiang, when resentment against ethnic Han domination of, well, pretty much everything in China comes to the surface, it is written off as "terrorism" (especially in Xinjiang, which has a large Muslim population), or as "splittism" (questioning China's borders), or as the actions of people filled with "foreign" ideas (such as human rights). No sane person, or no "good" Chinese citizen, the government seems to believe, would question why the dominant ethnic group should remain dominant in China. It's all just a continuation of the original civilizing mission that began the Chinese Empire in the first place.

While we're on the topic of China, let me bring in one more example that will show how our current flawed perceptions of history give us flawed approaches to diversity. In the ongoing debate over the status of Taiwan—the question is whether it belongs to China or is (or should be) independent—most people overlook the odd fact that no matter which side of the debate you are on,

Taiwan as it currently exists is quite clearly a product of multiple imperialisms. Starting in the seventeenth century, first the Dutch and then the Spanish tried to settle the island and use it as a trading outpost. The island, however, was not uninhabited. Several different groups of people already lived on the island, and those groups were not, as you might think, people from mainland China (linguistically and culturally, the earliest inhabitants of Taiwan have far more in common with Pacific Island cultures than with anything in China or Asia). When the Dutch and the Spanish weren't fighting each other, they were both doing what they could to battle the fierce resistance they met from the peoples already living on the island. Chinese involvement didn't start until later in the century. If at this point in the story you're thinking China got involved to remove the white imperialists from their territory, you'd be wrong. China certainly wanted to remove the European imperialist presence, but that's because China was going through an imperialist expansion of its own. If you were one of the indigenous populations in Taiwan in the seventeenth century, what you saw were three equally foreign imperialisms—one Dutch, one Spanish, and one Chinese—all battling each other over a territory that wasn't theirs to begin with and taking over your lands in the process (again, sound familiar?).

The Qing dynasty, which came to power in China in 1644, had become involved in Taiwan largely to stamp out the residue of anti-Qing resistance from Ming dynasty (previous dynasty) loyalists. Once that happened, Qing authorities weren't sure what they wanted to do with Taiwan, since it was notoriously difficult to govern (indigenous resistance). In the meantime, Chinese colonial settlers began to arrive to take over lands (for the record, these would have been undocumented immigrants). At one point, Qing authorities tried to *build a wall* to separate settlers from indigenous populations, fearing rebellion, but by the mid-eighteenth century any pretense that this was anything other than an imperialist colonization was removed and settlers from China flowed in at a steady rate, pushing indigenous populations onto marginal lands in the process (again, sound familiar?). Interestingly, the government of Taiwan recognizes the aboriginal populations as indigenous (*yuánzhùmín*, "original inhabitants") while the government of China does not (*Gaoshanzú*, "high mountain people").

If you're struggling at this point to see these three imperialisms in the same picture frame, then you are also seeing the problem I am getting at. The reason that so much of diversity discourse in America puts "white people" at the center as the sole problem to be fixed is because we have these distorted views of history that try to argue that history was going along nicely "until the white man came." That's a grotesque misreading of history. The very idea that Chinese imperialism could be an equal imperialism, or the very possibility that an "imperialism of color" could exist, compromises our whole approach to diversity. But it *should* compromise our whole approach to diversity because this whole approach is fundamentally flawed to begin with. We need a better reading of history if we have any hope of getting a better diversity.

Lucy in the sky with imperialist diamonds
We've left America for a bit to travel to other parts of the world, but think of how we would view these things if we transposed them back to the United States. In any moment when discussions of diversity cross with immigration reform, one of the first things that usually shows up in the discussion as evidence of how the "American Empire" is "completely racist" is the attempt to regulate and seal off the border between the United States and Mexico. The construction of the longest fence in North America—1,951 miles long—strengthened by the passage of the Secure Fence Act of 2006, is seen by many critics as a waste of taxpayer money and as a direct racist statement against persons of Mexican descent. But suppose the fence were renamed the Great Wall of America,

a marvel of engineering (there is talk now of a high-tech fenceless boundary that uses sophisticated sensors to detect movement across the border) and a testament to the great civilization of the United States. Suppose tour buses were driven to the border to display this testament to the greatness of America, and the need for a great country like America to keep foreigners out in order to protect our empire from the bad outsiders who might wish us harm. Imagine if during those tours, the tour guides praised movements and violent incidents in the United States that were anti-foreign in intent or were designed to keep members of minority races from coming to power. When you think of that, are you appalled? Disgusted? Angry? Offended? I would be too, but I am also equally offended when I see similar things anywhere in the world, including, as I have already discussed, in China.

Giant walls are rarely built for noble purposes, and as I have said over and over again, if we are going to get diversity right, then we have to get history right as well. If Imperial China and its Great Wall are seen as impressive achievements, then we will have to see Imperial Britain and Imperial America and every other similar entity (including the Berlin Wall) in the same positive light. Conversely, if you find the idea of British Imperialism or French Imperialism or the American Empire to be arrogant and shameful moments of history, with nothing redeeming to celebrate, then it is only appropriate that we see all other similar imperialist moments in the same critical light.

To reach even further back into history, we could go back to the time of what is considered by some to be our earliest human ancestor, who goes by the name of Lucy. Lucy, whose skeletal remains were unearthed in Ethiopia in 1974 and whose name is taken from the song "Lucy in the Sky with Diamonds" by The Beatles, dates back to around 3.2 million years ago, putting her in the species known as *Australopithecus afarensis*. I find it interesting to think of a time in world history when ethnicity had no meaning.

No discussion of Neanderthals, for instance, ever asks what race or ethnicity they might have had—they were just "all the same." They were inferior beings and human ancestors, chronological foreigners to us here living in the diversified present.

Why am I talking about this? Well, this might be a good moment to reflect upon where we came from, as in, where we *all* came from. It makes for an interesting experiment to read about the evolution of humans with the soundtrack of diversity playing in the background. Just as pretty much all imperialist histories interpret events in ways that flatter imperialists, especially since those histories are written by imperialists, a great deal of scientific writing unwittingly mimics the language of imperialist history. In an article about the rise of humans as top predator, for instance, we find that among the reasons for the rise of humans as the dominant species (that's right, humans are the dominant group, but remember, diversity tells us to resist and oppose dominant groups) was our "creative mind," meaning that our "large brains dreamed up ingenious technologies for killing and defleshing animals for food." In the same way that imperialist histories like to eliminate elements like luck or accident, many writers on this subject make it sound like humans intentionally evolved their own brains, as if somehow, shortly after the time of Lucy, human ancestors met as a group and said: "We need bigger brains, so let's get to work." Animals foolishly did not follow suit, which is why we can dominate them. In the same article, incidentally, we also find this gem of an insight: "Hunting also made us human in another respect. *H. sapiens* is unique among primates in having colonized every corner of the globe."[31] Colonialism, in other words, is what makes us human.

That particular article hints at the ability of humans to hunt, leading to better and more complex social bonds, but there is a

---

31 Kate Wong, "Rise of the Human Predator," *Scientific American* (April 2014), p. 51

more sinister side to this, too, which is that as humans developed more "ingenious" methods of killing, they just as quickly turned them on each other as they did on other animals. According to one analyst, the rise of humans was also the rise of an arms race, "making human groups one another's most dangerous predators." This article also argues that the rise of humans was more of an evolutionary accident, which, if true, means we can't bask in human glory too much.[32]

Yet another author refers to the rise of humans as "the most invasive species of all" and the "ultimate invader," largely based on our ability to create very lethal weapons and then work together to deploy them in creatively lethal ways. What I find interesting here is that, again, these are interpreted as positive traits, the things we clever humans did to colonize the world and subjugate everything else around us.[33] And for anyone thinking at least back then we lived in harmony with nature, we didn't. We left behind a whole host of devastating ecological changes, including the extinction of other species.

Of course, in the last stages of the evolution of modern humans, we have the story of how the Neanderthals eventually disappeared, and *Homo sapiens*—the supposedly new and improved and more intelligent and more civilized variant of humanity—conquered all. A great deal of academic writing on this transition has made Neanderthals out to be dumb brutes, which sets the stage for the rise of *Homo sapiens* ("sapiens" means wise), whose superior intelligence sent the inferior Neanderthals to the dustbin of extinction. However, according to at least one researcher, what made possible the rise and dominance of *Homo sapiens* was, as the

---

[32] Ian Tattersall, "If I Had a Hammer," *Scientific American* (September 2014), p. 58-59

[33] Curtis W. Marean, "The Most Invasive Species of All," *Scientific American* (August 2015), p. 33-39

previous articles have hinted, the invention of more lethal weapons through projectile technology, itself a result of the enhanced cognitive powers of *Homo sapiens*. This advanced martial technology gave *Homo sapiens* a decided advantage over Neanderthals in terms of warfare and hunting (incidentally, you'll never find an imperialist history that doesn't also include the development of more lethal weaponry and claims to superior intelligence). Eventually, *Homo sapiens* as a group was able to use that superior technology to control the resources needed by the Neanderthals to survive, or to simply dominate them through warfare (again, sound familiar?). In other words, Neanderthals didn't just disappear—we wise humans invaded and eliminated them. The conclusion of all of this turns out to be rather sobering news: modern humanity was born through the greatest act of collective imperialism and colonization ever witnessed in history.[34] In other words, no matter who you are or where you are from, if you are human, you are the product of at least one moment of imperialism. We've all got blood on our hands. That's right, we are all imperialists now.

The selective silence of history
If you're still having trouble understanding how our current facile vision of diversity renders us unable or unwilling to understand the complexity of human history, let me focus on one example for a moment to try to make this clear. The moment I will focus on is the colonization of Australia. As you take a moment to sigh and roll your eyes, thinking "here we go again, the White Man shows up to ruin everything," I've got some good news for you—I'm not talking about *that* colonization of Australia. I'm talking about the earlier colonization of Australia, the one undertaken

---

34 Kyle S. Brown *et al.*, "An early and enduring advanced technology originating 71,000 years ago in South Africa," *Nature* (November 7, 2012) at https://www.nature.com/articles/nature11660

by the groups that are now considered the aboriginal population (indigenous peoples) of Australia. Even if no other peoples were present when these groups came to Australia, we still refer to the process as colonization or colonialism. That earlier colonization took place, by a rough estimate, around 40-45,000 years ago.

In our current discussions of indigenous peoples, situated as it is in our current thoughts about white colonization and imperialism as the "moment when everything changed," we tend to believe that indigenous peoples are people who live in harmony with the land, people who were the original environmentalists, who lived responsibly and sustainably until white imperialism, with its capitalist commodification of the environment, arrogantly introduced environmental devastation in the name of so-called civilization. But recent studies have shown that the original human colonization of Australia was every bit as destructive to the Australian environment as the modern version.[35] Nearly every major indigenous (nonhuman) species was hunted to extinction, and human colonization also destroyed much of the natural environment, either through human-lit fire or through unsustainable methods of environmental overuse. Australia as it looks today is largely the result of the environmental devastation caused by the first human settlers. Scientists who undertook the research had to double-check and triple-check the results, largely because they had a hard time believing that humans, especially humans without access to anything like modern machinery, could cause so much mass destruction and extinction in such a short period of time (possibly less than 1,000 years).

We tend to leave animals out of our anthropocentric history of the world, seeing humans as the civilized winners who fought to the top of the food chain, which pretty much makes all nonhuman

---

35 Matt McGlone, "The Hunters Did It," *Science* 335/6075 (March 23, 2012) at http://science.sciencemag.org/content/335/6075/1452

species non-actors in the story, little more than living resources to be exploited for human use and on human terms. If we ever change our way of perceiving history in such a way, and find a way to include animal perspectives in global histories, human action won't come off as being quite as wise (*sapiens*) as we think. In this newly-revised history of the world, the chapter on the topic of imperialism won't start with the story of white Europeans, but rather will rather be titled "The First Wave of Destruction: Indigenous Imperialism and Colonization." If animals could write that part of the history, they'd use words like "faunacide" and "floracide," and when the story finally made it to the arrival of Europeans in Australia so many centuries later, most of the voices would be silent since they were wiped out long ago, in the first era of human colonization, the one when the indigenous people arrived. Oh, and from an animal perspective, *they're* the indigenous ones, not the humans.

Many a reader probably at some point in reading the last paragraph thought that I must be having a Berkeley moment, one in which the weed-infused fog has gently wafted across the bay and into my window, thus overwhelming my senses and leaving me typing with one hand while playing my bongo drum with the other. I can assure you that's not the case—I'm actually playing my bongo drum with both hands and typing with my feet—but in writing about this new perspective on human history I am actually suggesting a very serious challenge to our current views on humanity and diversity.

Consider this: it is as difficult for most people to see nonhuman animals as anything more than background scenery for the "central" story of human colonialism as it was for Christopher Columbus to see prior inhabitants of the Americas as anything more than background scenery for the "central" story of European exploration of the world. Other ideas that we now take (mostly) for granted were not that long ago seen as absurd and preposterous. As I write, almost exactly 150 years ago (in 1857), the US Supreme

Court denied personhood, citizenship, and freedom to Dred Scott simply because they were still unable to see that persons of African descent were every bit as human and every bit as entitled to constitutional rights and freedoms as anyone else. Ninety years ago, in 1927, five women from the Canadian province of Alberta challenged the Canadian Supreme Court with the simple question of whether the word "persons" in the British North America Act (which created the Dominion of Canada in 1867) included women. The Canadian Supreme Court stated quite clearly that the answer was *no*—only men had sufficient intelligence to be full legal persons, and only men could thus be responsible for their own affairs. Just less than 50 years ago, the 1969 Stonewall Riots became a landmark moment in the fight for gay rights as civil rights, but still, even in 1969, the phrase "marriage equality" would have made absolutely no sense to anyone. My point being that ideas that may strike you as absurd and preposterous now, in the present, may in fact actually be the cutting edge of history—the shape of things to come.

But back to the story of the colonization of Australia. One of the other reasons that researchers wanted to double-check and triple-check the results about indigenous environmental destruction is something that brings us back to the relationship between history and diversity. This particular set of findings doesn't reconcile well with the story that diversity as we currently have it wants to tell us: namely, that indigenous peoples lived in harmony with each other and with nature until the White Man arrived and ruined everything. It also doesn't paint a very flattering picture of humanity in general—looks like we've been ruining everything in wave after wave of human colonization and imperialism right from the start.[36] The arrival of the White Man is just one recent chapter that

---

36 This isn't just an issue of the past—it continues into the present. See Helen Briggs, "World's large carnivores being pushed off the map," *BBC News* (July

reads pretty much like all the previous ones. In the words of one of the researchers: "Like it or not, it's the truth, and it's time for us to all confront it."[37]

Those words are essential advice for getting diversity right. Simplistic ideas of diversity, ranging from who can or can't be racist to who is or isn't responsible for social injustice, create a selective silence in the way we read and write our collective histories. Histories that tell us what we need or want to believe in the present—for instance, that the White Man ruined the world—are rushed into print, one after another, but narratives that challenge us, that suggest an alternative vision of history that requires an alternative vision of diversity, are suppressed, censored, or written off as "fake news." History is forced into silence when we in fact need it to speak loudly and clearly. More than that, when history is finally allowed to speak loudly and clearly, we ourselves need to do something truly revolutionary—we need to listen carefully and think lucidly.

One last point to make here. More than a few people might think that in pointing out that the aboriginal colonization of Australia was a highly destructive process I am somehow disparaging aboriginal cultures, or perhaps suggesting that we shouldn't care too much for what happened to aboriginal cultures when the White Man finally did arrive, that perhaps they "deserved" what they got. Nothing could be further from the truth. Harkening back to an earlier point I made about *negative equality*, there is something empowering about using the same critical lens to view aboriginal cultures as I would to view European cultures or any other culture for that matter. If we do anything otherwise, it amounts to differential treatment, and differential treatment is a

---

15, 2017) at http://www.bbc.com/news/science-environment-40596729

37 "'Humans killed off Australia's giant beasts'," *BBC News* (March 24, 2012) at http://www.bbc.com/news/science-environment-17488447

form of unequal treatment, the exact opposite of what diversity is supposed to provide. Being equally critical of all cultures and histories, for both the positive and negative things, is actually a form of equal respect, and equal respect is a form of empowerment. To point out the destructiveness of the aboriginal colonization of Australia, for instance, does not in any way mitigate the trauma or excuse the misguided policy of the Stolen Generations, in which aboriginal children in Australia were forcibly adopted into white families to "civilize" them and hasten assimilation. But silencing history in convenient ways to fulfill a political agenda in the present isn't going to give us justice either. If it gives us anything, it will be more injustice in the short term and endless grief in the long term. No one should want that.

How to be wrong: the historical travesty of the post-colonial
To return us to the present, one of the by-products of this obsessive focus on the colonial—by which I mean an emphatic focus on *European* imperialism while trying to minimize or occlude other imperialisms—that transfuses directly into debates about diversity is the idea of the "post-colonial." As a chronological marker, it simply means, as its name implies, anything that comes after the historical period of the colonial (it gets confusing here sometimes because colonial and imperial refer to the same thing but there is no such term as post-imperial). Embedded into the idea of the post-colonial is much more than just chronology. It also contains the emotional amalgamation of all of the difficulties created in the aftermath of (European) colonialism, and the most important of these difficulties are the ones that relate to identity. To be "post-colonial"—and yes, people actually refer to themselves as post-colonials—is to have an identity that is irresolvably complex, due to the oppressively distortive forces set in motion by colonialism itself. Much as history has been assumed—erroneously, as I have argued—to have been authentic and organic until (European)

colonialism and imperialism came along and changed what should have been into what shouldn't have been, those who were the victims of this historical process lost the identity they should have had (the authentic identity) and were forced to take on new identities not of their own choosing. With the loss of the old and presumably real identity, which is permanently irrecoverable, and with the pressure to assimilate to the colonizer's identity, which is permanently unattainable (for the colonized), there were whole groups of people around the world who in the aftermath of colonization had lost their old identities but could not create new ones. These were identity victims who were caught in-between, with nebulous and indistinct identities, unable to go back to the past and unable to find a point of arrival in the future. Post-colonials are therefore people whose identities are permanently caught in-between, neither here nor there. The colonizers, meanwhile, as in, The (White) Europeans, never lost their authenticity and so they get to enjoy their real and unproblematic identity, without suffering any of the identity-based traumas they inflicted on other people. In this context, diversity is seen as one possibility to end the interminable indeterminacy of post-colonial identity. Diversity finally affords a chance to recover the authenticity that was lost, a chance to hold the colonizer accountable for the destruction of authentic identities, upon which the idea of the post-colonial is based.

If you are wondering how all of this happened, there is no shortage of explanations. These explanations emanate from the field of what is called post-colonial studies, an entire field devoted to explaining how colonialism was the most important and most destructive event in the history of the world. How important was the arrival of Europeans to world history? So important, says the conceptual basis of post-colonial studies, that all of human history can be divided into three basic epochs: pre-colonial (when all was authentic), colonial (when all was devastated), and post-colonial (when all is distorted). One example of how the field of post-colonialism explains the deleterious transformation of identity under colonialism, and this is just one chosen from among many, is through the metaphor of *infantilization*. In this theory, the European colonizers showed up in various soon-to-be-colonized locations and positioned themselves as superior to the native population, much as a parent would position themselves in relation to a child (and much as *Homo sapiens* would position themselves in relation to Neanderthals). Over time—and post-colonial theory is very weak on precisely how this happened—the colonized populations took on their subordinate roles and were therefore transformed into child-like beings by the colonizers, who increasingly became more secure and more domineering in their self-appointed role as "parents" to the colonized "children." Colonialism rendered colonized people into "child-like" beings, and the effort of the post-colonial has been to regain dignity by re-establishing the equality of adulthood among the people of the world.[38] Diversity programs often link themselves to the post-colonial idea with the suggestion of creating policies that are supposed to establish equality of identity in place of colonial hierarchies that saw some as superior and adult-like (European colonizers) and others as inferior and child-like (the globally colonized).

Like all theories, there is an element of heuristic cogency here that seems satisfyingly complete. Also like all theories, when you take the time to look a little closer at things, you begin to discern gaps and holes and imperfections that call into question some parts, if not *all* parts, of the explanatory edifice. One begins to marvel more at the child-like simplicity of post-colonial explanations than at the alleged child-like constructions of colonial powers. Post-colonial theory, for instance, is noticeably weak on motive and agency. How was it so easy for a group of foreigners

---

38 See, for instance, as an early example, Ashis Nandy, *The Intimate Enemy* (1990)

(the colonizers) to show up in other lands and convince people to accept their inferiority? How did the colonizers know so well what to do, and how did the colonized not see what was happening? If the structures created by the colonizers were so insidious and hateful, why did so many of the colonized population take so readily to them? Indeed, why do so many people in colonized countries still take to those structures today, long after the colonizers have gone? For my part, I would argue it this way: post-colonialism is equally complicit in creating the child-like persona of colonized identities. In short, *post-colonial theory infantilizes the post-colonial mind.*

To be child-like, for instance, is to be innocent. We hold adults fully accountable for their actions—and post-colonial theory certainly does that with the colonizers, so they are seen as adults. But the colonized peoples of the world are often seen by post-colonial scholars and activists as not responsible for anything that happened, especially if it is something negative. Like children, they were and still are too innocent and too unaware to be responsible for their actions. We already saw earlier how with negative things like racism, in formerly colonized countries this is considered an unfortunate legacy of colonial rule and not something that people in colonized countries would have done themselves. When colonial rulers are racist, we hold them fully accountable for these views. When formerly-colonized peoples are equally racist, post-colonial theory renders them into a child-like state where they remain unaware that racism is wrong and therefore are not really responsible for their racism. Post-colonial theory then spawns histories around these ideas that parse the complex array of events of the colonial period and produce histories that reclaim the good parts as authentic and native and reject the bad parts (such as racism) as inauthentic and colonially-imposed. It's a No-Child-Left-Behind perspective on world history: the child-like peoples of the post-colonial world can write child-like histories that are embarrassingly simple in their selective retelling of events, and each of those histories is awarded three-gold stars and a blue ribbon, no matter how implausible or poorly-written they may be. Does it reverse and redress the crimes of colonialism? Not at all. Does it help us understand the complex ways that historical moments like colonialism occur? Not in the least. Does it help us improve the ways that different populations view one another, that is, does it create a history that gives us some sense of how we might do a better job of positioning ourselves among others? Not even close.

How to get away with genocide
To offer one specific example of how this plays out, let us look to one of the more tragic moments of recent history—the 1994 genocide that occurred in Rwanda. In a paroxysm of personal and collective violence that the mind and heart both struggle to comprehend, over 800,000 people were slaughtered in the span of 100 days, nearly all of them hacked to death in machete attacks. Most but not all of the victims of the genocide came from the ethnic Tutsi community, a minority community that was also the dominant community in Rwanda (that is, the minority community held the preponderance of cultural, social, and political power). Nearly all analysts approach the genocide from the broader perspective of post-colonial theory, which means that the genocide itself is explained as a by-product of Belgian colonial rule in Rwanda, a sort of tragic post-colonial blood-letting created by forces set in motion by the (white) colonizing powers and over which Rwandans had little or no control. In Mahmood Mamdani's book on the genocide, tellingly entitled *When Victims Become Killers*, he offers a succinct and eloquent version of this argument: "The origin of the violence is connected to how Hutu and Tutsi were constructed as political identities by the colonial state, Hutu as indigenous and Tutsi as alien. The reason for continued violence between Hutu and Tutsi…is connected with the failure of Rwandan nationalism

to transcend the colonial construction of Hutu and Tutsi as native and alien."[39] By this reckoning, had there been no colonialism in Rwanda, there would have been no genocide.

I find these types of arguments not merely unsatisfying but to a certain extent offensive to the victims of the genocide. If the manipulation of identities by colonial rulers created genocide, then why hasn't there been a genocide in every formerly colonized country? In one of the very few books to discuss the motivations of those who killed in the genocide, Jean Hatzfeld's *Machete Season* (2006), you will hear many disturbing reasons why people decided to participate and kill others—they were just caught up in the fervor, they were following orders, they were under peer pressure, they were willing to do the "work" (killing) for free beer and food (not kidding on the last point)—but what you won't hear are discussions of how colonial manipulations of identity made them kill people. These were not child-like people who made decisions for which they cannot be held accountable: these are adults who made decisions that some, but disturbingly not all of them, lived to regret. Post-colonial theory cannot adequately explain why so many ethnic Hutu chose to participate in the genocide. But the more important question that post-colonial perspectives fail to answer is why so many more Hutu chose *not* to participate. Moral choice and agency were clearly possible. Nor can such stories explain why the genocide occurred in 1994 and not 1992 or 1985 or any other time. If the genocide were created by colonially-imposed racism, then the genocide would have started long ago and most likely would never have stopped.

It is tempting and perhaps gratifying to believe in a simplified story where the colonizer of the past shoulders the blame for everything in the present, including genocide, but those explanations

---

39 Mahmood Mamdani, *When Victims Become Killers: Colonialism, Nativism, and the Genocide in Rwanda* (2001), 34

can never account for the wide variation of post-colonial experience that happens in the present. Indeed, many of the stories of the killers in Rwanda match those of killers who participated in other genocides where colonialism was not a factor at all. Time and time again, those Hutus who engaged in the killings often stated that they had lived side by side as friends with their Tutsi neighbors, but then in 1994 everything changed. If they had lived side by side for so many years as friends, then clearly the murderous racism attributed to Belgian colonialism could not be a causal factor. Also consider the fact that only 1 in 5 Rwandans actually participated in the genocidal killing, which means that 4 out of 5, or 80%, knew it was wrong and were clearly not mindlessly following the identity-based manipulations of the Belgian colonizers.[40] There is simply too much evidence that individual choices could be and were made in the context of the Rwandan genocide, and it is doing no one any favors to look upon the Rwandan people as child-like natives who were not really aware of their actions in the ambient fog of post-colonial history.

Individual agency shows the bankruptcy of post-colonial theory in countless ways. Many a post-colonial scholar and many a post-colonial nationalist have made similar arguments about how imperialism is to blame for so many negative things, but here again, there is too much variation in outcomes and inconsistency in evidence to argue that colonialism and imperialism are to blame. In India, for instance, the nuclear weapons program that is the source of so much nationalist pride is always emphasized as an *indigenous* weapons program (meaning India alone takes credit for its accomplishment), but if the discussion switches to India's tragic levels of poverty, then one hears explanations that start with

---

40 Omar Shahabudin McDoom, "Who killed in Rwanda's genocide? Microspace, social influence and individual participation in intergroup violence," *Journal of Peace Research* 50/4 (2013): 453-467

"The British are responsible..." and so forth. No one ever talks about India's indigenous poverty. Both India and Singapore were British colonies, for instance, but the outcomes could not be more different: India has struggled with massive amounts of extreme poverty while Singapore—without even an agricultural sector of its own—has managed to find economic success and become one of the most dynamic economies in Asia. In India, you will hear repeated references to how poverty was created by the British. In Singapore, you will hear references to how wealth is created by good policy—colonialism is irrelevant (and indeed, the economists I talk with in Singapore are inclined to point out that the reasons for India's poverty are bad policy and corruption in the present). Even within sub-Saharan Africa, there are too many different variations in outcomes from the same colonial starting point to ascribe everything to the white colonial moment. Liberia and Botswana could not be more different, but the government of Botswana makes it quite clear that it is carefully crafted policy—choice and action in the present—that is responsible for this. And concerning genocide itself, I find it quite revealing that when it comes to the genocide in Cambodia (1975-9), though Cambodia was a formerly a French colony, no one is blaming the French for the genocide. At the genocide trials being conducted in Cambodia (which will soon come to a close), the focus of the courts has been on what individuals chose to do in the moment of genocide, and not on how their post-colonial identity made them victims who became killers. Clearly, something far beyond colonialism must be involved to explain these different outcomes—genocide here but not there, wealth there but not here—and this seems to render the idea of the post-colonial obsolete and irrelevant (if not offensive) even at its very moment of birth.

So to return to the situation in Rwanda: does it really help us to return to the colonial past? Does it help us to think that the identities that were in play during the horrific genocide in Rwanda were created by outside (European) colonial forces over which ordinary Rwandans had little or no control? Not only do I think that these approaches are not helpful, but they might in fact be harmful, largely because they end up creating a rhetorical assembly-line for the kinds of excuses that dictators and genocidal killers find remarkably convenient. After all, the post-colonial approach tells us that colonized peoples are not fully accountable for their actions due to their persistent and ongoing victimization at the hands of colonial history. It isn't by accident that every time Robert Mugabe, recently-deposed leader of Zimbabwe, is criticized for his brutal suppression of the democratic opposition in his country and for his flagrant abuse of human rights, his ad nauseam response is that he is doing what he has to do to resist the "re-colonization" of Zimbabwe by the Europeans, who apparently invented human rights with the goal of oppressing Africa down (don't think on that too long—your brain will start to erode). Post-colonial theory is like a gift-wrapped get-out-of-jail-free-forever card for some of the worst people in all of humanity. At the end of the day, the infantilization and moral laxity created by post-colonial theory gives us not justice but rather more racism, more dictatorship, and more genocide, among other things, by ensuring and insisting that we do not hold non-Western peoples accountable for their actions. This forever puts the people in formerly colonized countries into a child-like identity in relation to the rest of the world. The best way to bring justice to the post-colonial world, and the best way to allow diversity to move forward, whether in America or anywhere else in the world, is to shut down the post-colonial loophole. We're all adults, just as we're all imperialists.

Another post on the post-colonial
Although the idea of being post-colonial is something that we associate with one moment in time—the time when European colonizers went out in search of a world to colonize—if we return to a

point I made earlier about opening up all of history for equal scrutiny, we quickly bump up against a reality that is as discomfiting as it is scintillating. Since we know that imperialism and colonialism have taken place throughout human history—indeed, as I mentioned earlier there is the very real possibility that human history itself was only made possible by the imperialism of *homo sapiens*—then clearly, there must also be post-colonial moments scattered throughout history as well. That is, post-colonialism, if we are to retain the word and the concept at all, should not be confined to just one specific moment in time or applied to one specific group of peoples. In a broader historical context, for instance, both the United States and Great Britain can legitimately be considered post-colonial countries. American identity and the American political landscape were forged out of resistance to British colonial policy, a resistance that culminated in a war of independence and a definitive act of decolonization. All Americans are therefore to some degree or other post-colonial people. There are plenty of people who would balk if not bristle at the very suggestion that Americans could be a post-colonial people, and would be quick to point out that only certain minority groups could lay legitimate claim to that title (interesting how many times people use the term "post-colonial" when they really mean "people of color"). The dominant group can only be a colonizer, they would say, never the colonized. In this context, I would only point out the oddity in this peculiar framing of American identities: how many people in America are also descendants of Spanish colonizers?

Britain's post-colonial identity is even more vexing and beguiling, largely for the way it exposes the fundamental flaws in the very idea that post-colonialism is an experience and an identity-marker that applies only to one group of people from only one point in historical time. For those whose sense of history is a bit rusty and are struggling to think of when Britain might have been colonized, I would direct your attention back to the Anglo-Saxon period (Anglo-Saxon identity is itself a combination of colonizing populations), when Vikings from Scandinavia began a series of predations against Britain, sometimes creating colonies and sometimes laying waste to whole villages and ransacking monasteries (and killing the monks inside them). The reign of King Cnut "the Great" (1016-1035) marked a particular moment of imperial consolidation when a Danish and therefore foreign ruler reigned supreme in Britain, much as Queen Victoria reigned over India when it was a colony of Britain (actually even more so since King Cnut directly ruled Britain in the country itself). The colonial experience left Britain devastated, colonized, and subjugated. Place-names still to this day bear their imposed colonial origins, and clearly, British identity was transformed forever into something it would not otherwise have been. If post-colonial theory were correct, then Britain would see this moment as the point where its own authentic and organic history went off course, when authentic British identity was lost because of the predations of the foreign colonizers. So why aren't people in Britain clamoring to recapture their "real" identity or clamoring to make Scandinavia pay for its colonial theft of British riches? Why aren't we writing books about British imperialism in India with titles like *When Victims Become Colonizers* and not holding the British fully accountable for their actions due to the dislocations of the violent and brutal history of colonization inflicted upon them?

There are two common answers given for this, both of them equally wrong and equally misguided. Both answers do, however, speak to how the use of post-colonial theory impinges upon and grotesquely distorts the relationship between history and diversity in the present. The first is the argument that Britain's colonization happened too long ago to matter in the present. This argument reveals a fundamental flaw in all arguments that try to link present-day initiatives for enhanced diversity with compensation for past acts of historical injustice: how far back in history should we go?

The question is not an idle one, and the lack of a specific answer makes it impossible to link diversity with history in any constructive way. The current answer, as we have seen, is to go back only to the moment of (European) imperialism and look no further, but there is absolutely no compelling or convincing argument to make that moment our only moment of historical inquiry. If we are going to go back to the nineteenth century, why not go back to the eighteenth century? If we are going to look at the crimes of European imperialism, why not look at the crimes of other imperialisms, too? Unless someone can come up with a specific date, beyond which history does not matter for contemporary justice, *and* create a compelling argument for why we should limit our inquiry only to that place and time, then we will have to let history go by the wayside—that is, we will have to *delink* history and diversity. That would harken back to the *Grutter* decision from the US Supreme Court, which effectively delinked diversity from history by arguing that diversity (through affirmative action) should focus on integrating present-day social relations and not on creating historical justice.

The second argument is a bit more troublesome. I will articulate this argument through the actions and words of a student who quite literally and angrily stormed out of a classroom discussion when I merely suggested the idea that Britain could be seen as a post-colonial country. She eventually returned, still fuming, but only to make a brief point: the Danish and the British were both just white people, and white people colonizing white countries, if in fact it actually occurred (which she doubted), was just white people with white problems. (For those who don't know, "white problems" is a colloquial phrase referring to the problems that white people face that aren't actually serious problems—implying that white people are too privileged to have real problems.) In other words, the Danish and the British, since they were both white and European, were pretty much the same thing. Having one of them attack and colonize the other amounted pretty much to white people moving from one white part of Europe to the other. And so, white people attacking and killing other white people was just not all that important. White people moving out of Europe and colonizing non-white people, on the other hand, was a historical crime called imperialism. Those countries could be post-colonial, but *not* Britain.

If you are reading this and are inclined to agree with any of these points in any way, then allow me to introduce you to my good friends, the Koreans. If this student's argument—and she is not alone in this perspective, trust me—has any merit to it, that is, if imperialism is wrong only if it involves one identity group venturing sufficiently far away from home and colonizing "foreigners," then the Japanese expansion into Korea, the annexation of Korea to Japan in 1910, and all of the related violence and destruction it caused—including the forced recruitment of the "Comfort Women" (Korean women forced to service Japanese men in military brothels)—all of this is just crying over spilt milk apparently. After all, the historical and cultural similarities between Japanese and Koreans are at least as close if not closer than those between Danes and Brits, so according to this argument, it wasn't really even imperialism at all. It was just Asians moving from one part of Asia to another—Asians attacking other Asians, which just gave us more Asians. Just "Asian problems," right?

Or how about the Japanese occupation of Manchuria in China? The horrible violence of the events known as the Rape of Nanking? If the student's argument is correct, then there was no Japanese Empire, these events don't matter, and the continuing anger that China and South Korea feel toward Japan's historical actions is unfounded. It was all just Asians interacting with Asians in Asian ways.

Do you feel your blood beginning to boil at this point? Do you find this offensive? Insulting? Disrespectful? Ignorant? If you answered all of the above, then three cheers for caring enough to start the process of rethinking history. Next step: Read what happened in Britain, starting with the invasions of the Saxons and going through to the invasions of the Viking colonizers—pay attention to the cultural devastation, the rape, the pillage, the plunder, the taking of land. Note that it did as much to destroy native culture and identity in Britain as did any aspect of (European) imperialism in non-European lands. Then imagine what it must have been like trying to live through it. If you think it happened too long ago to matter, then all I ask—again—is that you give us a specific date that divides human history neatly into two parts: the part that matters (we care enough to seek justice) and the part that doesn't (injustice is not a problem). So far, no one has been able to do that, and for good reason: *it cannot be done.* Any date will always be too arbitrary and too meaningless. The artifice of a pre-colonial, colonial, and post-colonial world must fall before diversity can succeed.

Everywhere you look, you can find unexpected counter-examples to break us free from the incessant obsession with the simplified history of imperialism. Finland, for instance, was invaded and colonized by other countries (Sweden and Russia), its people pushed to the bottom of the hierarchy and looked down upon as savages. It endured colonial famine and a violent war of liberation that then turned into a civil war that devastated much of the country in the 1930s. Finland is just as much a post-colonial country as, say, India, yet the outcomes could not be more different. Like Singapore, Finland made different choices in its post-colonial period. Among other things, they managed go from being one of the poorest and most corrupt countries in Europe (in the immediate aftermath of colonization) to one of the least corrupt and most economically vibrant countries in the world.

What these examples tell us—and there are many others like these—is that the link between history, identity, and imperialism is something we need to rethink from the ground up. If diversity is designed to give identity-based justice in the present, and if the injustices that diversity is designed to redress stem from history, then we need to open up our historical inquiries as widely and as fairly as possible, and we need to dispense with the idea that (European) imperialism changed the world from what it should have truly been (authentic) to what it tragically became (inauthentic). Diversity cannot reverse history. History changes all the time—that is what history is by definition—and identities change along with it. We are all as authentic as we would otherwise be.

Naming history: a quick example
It might seem like all of this gesticulating about post-colonial identities is something that only a bunch of academic troglodytes conjure up in order to appear relevant and/or intelligent, usually failing at both. But I can assure you that this type of identity-based irredentism—of trying to reclaim an identity that was allegedly lost due to historical events—can be found pretty much everywhere one looks. Since we have been spending so much time discussing India, let's continue that conversation a bit more.

In 1995, the state-level government of Maharashtra, in the western part of India, decided to rename the city of Bombay. The political party behind this decision was the Shiv Sena, a right-wing political party with deep Hindu nationalist roots, which means that their political platform contains a strong desire to reclaim and re-establish what they see as India's Hindu roots (which were lost due to foreign invasions—foreign in this case meaning anything non-Hindu). India is more authentic, they believe, the closer it comes to its Hindu origins—a clear example of chronological narcissism at work. Because Hinduism and Indian-ness are considered by the Shiv Sena to be one and the same, it stands to reason that anything that is non-Hindu and anything that is foreign must somehow be a force that takes India away from what it otherwise would and should have been. In other words, diversity for the Shiv Sena creates a *loss* of authenticity. To take India one step closer to its authentic identity, as conceived by the Shiv Sena at least, the Shiv Sena initiated a move to change the name of Bombay to Mumbai. Bombay, they argued, was a "foreign" name with colonial origins. On the other hand, Mumbai was the authentic word used for the city in the regional language of Maharashtra, which is Marathi. By renaming the city Mumbai, the Shiv Sena argued that they were erasing the last vestiges of colonialism from the city and reclaiming the authentic past.

No one has ever accused a government anywhere in the world of being too smart or too competent, but this example from the Shiv Sena offers us a glimpse into just how pervasive this idea of reversing history to reclaim identity is. As you can imagine, however, there are some problems with the Shiv Sena's project. In the first place, to rename the city Mumbai is to merely replace the Anglicized pronunciation of the city with a Marathi-language pronunciation. This is to confuse phonological revision with substantive revision. It would be a bit like changing the name of the city of Des Moines to Demoyne and arguing that by removing the French spelling and pronunciation, America became more authentic and more American.

Had the Shiv Sena done its homework a bit better, they would also have known that the English name Bombay came from the previous name for the area, Bom Bahia, which in Portuguese means "Beautiful Bay." The Portuguese had originally acquired the island for themselves and later ceded the territory to the British, and so yes, there is a colonial action at the center of this. But before anyone starts foaming at the mouth over the role of imperialism, one has to also consider that the lands that were ceded to the Portuguese were legally ceded because the local Indian ruler who originally owned them had invited Portuguese intervention because he feared the growing power of yet another imperial power in the region: the Mughal Empire (which was decidedly non-European but still very imperialist). If you are having a "wait… what?" moment right now, then take a moment to understand that yes, India's cultural and social and political landscape has been transformed by other, non-European empires. More on that in a moment.

When the Portuguese acquired the islands, they named them Bom Bahia ("beautiful bay"), which the British eventually Anglicized that into Bombay. Marathi-language pronunciation had always been closer to Mumbai, so the only thing actually accomplished by the Shiv Sena campaign was a phonological change to reflect local pronunciation of what is still a foreign, imperially-derived word. Nevertheless, in the state of Maharashtra, the move was greeted with a certain amount of fanfare: the colonial had been erased, so the post-colonial could get to the business of reclaiming lost identities. What I find interesting about the whole endeavor is that Mumbai itself as a city was left untouched. I mean, if you really wanted to erase the vestiges of imperialism, you would have to bring in a phalanx of bulldozers and other forms of heavy demolition equipment and destroy the entire infrastructure of the city, at a loss of hundreds of billions of dollars (Mumbai real estate rivals and often exceeds even Manhattan prices). Once the city has been completely dismantled, along with the Bollywood film industry (based as it is on Western musical genres of film imported during the colonial era), and once the landscape had been returned to the small cluster of villages next to a mosquito-infested (and malaria-infested), swampy body of water—then and only then can you rightfully claim to have dismantled the colonial presence and legacy for Mumbai.

(On a side note, given the discussion earlier of Mohamed Atta's hatred of skyscrapers in Aleppo as symbols of foreign and colonial rule, Mumbai is also home to the largest private residence in the world—a 16-story skyscraper that is the home of one of India's wealthiest entrepreneurs. What Atta hated as a symbol of the colonial and foreign West, Mumbai welcomes as a symbol of success.)

Nevertheless, so deeply embedded is the orthodox belief that erasing (or pretending to erase) any part of the colonial vestige reveals and restores some lost element of authentic identity, other cities in India soon followed suit—with similarly misinformed results. In 1996, the city of Madras, in the southern state of Tamil Nadu, officially renamed itself Chennai, with similar fanfare to Mumbai's renaming and with similar boasts about somehow making the city more authentic by recapturing a part of the pre-colonial past. Calcutta, too, was renamed Kolkata in 2001 by the state-level government in West Bengal, in order to recapture a more authentic name that was presumably in place before the British arrived.

One could argue that the renaming of cities in India—and many others have followed suit since Mumbai and Chennai—to recapture some conjured and evocative moment from the pre-colonial past, when identity was presumably "real," is just a harmless bit of political pomposity. But it speaks to the impulsively seductive power of the idea that there is this one moment in history, the moment of (European) imperialism, when everything in the world went horribly off course, and the almost messiah-like belief that with sustained and arduous efforts all that was lost can somehow be returned and all will be set right. Fortunately, no persons were harmed during the renaming of cities in India (though India is no stranger to identity-based violence), whereas for Mohammed Atta and others like him, the belief that the colonial moment had "ruined" what was pure and authentic in his cultural homeland transformed into a murderous hatred toward the alleged home of the thieves of his dream of identity-based purity: the West. The idea of the post-colonial feeds this insatiable beast of an idea by lending undeserved and unjustifiable credence to the belief that the great rift in human history created by the aberration of Western imperialism and colonialism somehow altered and distorted the identities of non-Western cultures from what they should have been, both past and present. The energy devoted to reclaiming and re-establishing those identities, of finding the El Dorado of one's authentic identity by reversing the presumed damage of one moment's historical gravity—the arrival of the white man—all of that is misplaced and wasted energy. The goal should not be to reverse history but to rethink it, and the first order of business is to abandon the idea that being post-colonial means anything exceptional or, quite frankly, anything at all. It's another crutch, another set of training wheels that holds back the possibility of meaningful diversity, in the West or anywhere else in the world for that matter. Once the moment of European colonialism and imperialism is shown to be not an aberration but a seamless transition in a story already filled with devastation and destruction, chapter after inexorable chapter—once that idea is deprived of its gravity and the post-colonial notion summarily dismissed from the catalog of available identities, only then can we speak of historical justice and meaningful identities. Only then.

Dividing and conquering history
One final stereotype that emerges from this grotesque overemphasis on Western colonialism as the most villainous moment in human history is summed up in the phrase "divide and conquer." This phrase, more of a cliché really, is usually said with a slight roll of the eyes, as if to call attention to how utterly sinister and devious the whole imperial project was. The divide-and-conquer idea refers to the putative ability of Western imperialists to show up in situations of presumed multicultural harmony—the pre-colonial times when diversity among different groups just naturally occurred without any difficulties—and convinced people who had gotten along for thousands of years to suddenly hate each other. First you divide these previously united populations, through some

sort of chicanery that apparently only Westerners are capable of, and then you conquer them. This idea is attractive to many in the present because it plays into the idea that diversity is something that the non-West always had—before the white man came—and so diversity in the present focuses on how non-Western peoples, or "communities of color" as the mistaken rhetoric goes, can re-establish that natural pre-colonial affinity that was somehow broken apart by the arrival of Western imperialism. This is one of the main reasons why, at least in America, when we speak of diversity programs, we really mean programs aimed at communities from non-Western identity backgrounds. White people don't have ethnicities—they're just imperialists.

Once again, if we had a better history to inform our ideas about diversity, we would see quite clearly that this idea is insipid nonsense. Through a clearer lens, one not caked with the vestigial residue of wistfulness and melancholy for long-lost but ultimately imaginary identities, we would see that the "classic divide and conquer" attributed to Western imperialism is either the "standard divide and conquer" carried out by pretty much every culture and society throughout all of human history or, more accurately, "easy to conquer because deep divisions were already present." We like to simplify things and use sentences like "when Britain colonized India" or "when Britain invaded India," but the actually process was quite different from that and at the same time *not* different from what other local rulers in India were already doing on their own. When "the British" arrived in India, they arrived as part of a private trading company called the East India Company, not as representatives of the kingdom of Great Britain. And the first plots of land they received were acquired quite legally, as gifts or concessions from local rulers who appreciated the expansion of local trade the East India Company provided, largely because it would give them extra money and hence extra autonomy from other rulers in India *who were already a part of pre-existing empires* (such as the Mughal Empire in the north or the Vijayanagara Empire in the south). Keep in mind also that in the seventeenth and eighteenth centuries, the very idea of India as a country did not exist, so we also cannot say that when "the British" showed up, "the Indians" did not understand what these foreigners were up to. Local rulers in India certainly saw the British traders as foreign, but no more foreign than traders from other parts of the world and even from other parts of what is now India.

The reason we do not have narratives that depict the complexity of historical interaction is because of the way we have distorted those narratives through erroneous beliefs about our identities, past and present. The more accurate version of history—"easy to conquer because society was already deeply divided"—undermines cherished beliefs in the present about unified identities in the past, identities that were "lost" when the white man came. This projecting of what we wish for in the present back into the past probably does more damage for the viability of a vibrant and constructive diversity than nearly any other single factor. The idea of ethnic and nationalistic solidarity in the past, or the lamenting of things that never could have happened anyway—oh, why didn't India pull together as a nation and resist the British?—is a bad idea from start to finish. Yet the desire persists to see things this way, to see for instance how the Spaniards "broke apart" Latin America (it was never united to begin with), largely because they support narratives in the present about the need for various ethnic groups to stick together and rebuild communities (even if those communities never actually existed in the past). If such groups do not stick together and "stick to their own kind," the argument goes, then they are conceding the ultimate victory to the (European) colonizers. Racial and ethnic solidarity in the present is therefore justified on the grounds of "resistance" to the imperialist injustice of the past.

I also find the other part of the whole premise a bit puzzling, the part that says that the white man showed up and was able to discern everything clearly and quickly in his new environment, even more clearly and quickly than the people who had lived in the environment long before the moment when the white man arrived (incidentally, white women also participated, but we always conveniently leave that out). Considering that one of the things singled out for offensiveness in the whole process of colonization is the way that the Western imperialists attributed a superior intelligence and a more lucid perceptiveness to themselves, it seems very odd to me that on this point, those two things—a superior intelligence and a more lucid perceptiveness—are happily attributed by the colonized to the colonizer. If the idea that the white man arrived and somehow manipulated local feuds to gain power overlooks the extent to which those pre-existing local feuds were the central problem, then the idea that the Western imperialists were able to manipulate those local feuds more successfully than other local rulers who were attempting the same thing merely puts the Western imperialists on top of the hierarchy as the smartest bunch around. Granted, it's not a good hierarchy to be on top of, but nevertheless, it seems to confirm in a very puzzling and disturbing way one of the central self-attributed claims of Western imperialism.

The other way of seeing things, of looking at the arrival of Western imperialism as just one more chapter in an ongoing and mostly sordid story that started long before the arrival of the white man, makes far better historical sense. But it deprives us of the ability to claim that diversity in the present is somehow intended to be an act of resistance against the injustices of the past. Coming together and promoting ethnic and group-based solidarity does not repudiate the injustices of the imperial past, but merely replicates them. Once we remove ourselves from the identity-based shackles of our dysfunctional and disremembered pasts, what we lose in terms of chronological narcissism we will gain in terms of present-day diversity. The more we let go of the vision of an idyllic and utopian past, the more we have to work with, collectively, in our shared and ever-changing present. The future is unwritten, but what becomes of the future, at least as far as diversity is concerned, will depend on whether or not we are brave enough now to face the past and rewrite all of it—word by word, moment by moment.

Disfiguring and reconfiguring the past
It is easy to lose sight of all this maneuvering about events that happened long ago as so much esoteric graffiti on the otherwise pristine walls of the vaunted ivory tower, but it is important to remember—continuously—that all of this plays out with its own "street cred" in everyday action and everyday policy in institutions at home and around the world. One of the central projects of the United Nations at its founding in 1945, for instance, was to initiate and oversee the project of global decolonization. Decolonization in this case refers to the process of breaking apart existing empires to allow the colonized peoples of the world their first taste of autonomous freedom and their first chance at self-determination in the aftermath of colonialism. Yet, the United Nations then, as so many voices in the cacophonic choir of diversity still do today, thought that there was only one type of colonialism and imperialism that existed in the world, and that was the variety practiced by the West. One by one, European empires were put under intense pressure to dismantle and decolonize. Other empires, for instance the Japanese empire, which was every bit as invasive, expansive, and destructive as anything that Europe put forth, were left intact, or resolved separately in peace negotiations following World War II. It was not seen as a substantive empire worthy of the decolonization process by the United Nations, largely because it wasn't a Western empire.

Some Western countries postponed the process almost indefinitely—France unilaterally took French Polynesia and New Caledonia off the decolonization list, making both of those countries some of the last outposts of Western empires still to remain in the world (though the Noumea Accords will require a referendum on independence in New Caledonia by 2018, and French Polynesia was put back on the UN decolonization list in 2013, much to the anger of France). But other empires, specifically non-European ones such as the Chinese empire, were left completely untouched. When Tibet approached the United Nations seeking independence shortly after the UN's founding, the UN did not accept the claim because no European empire was involved. Indeed, when the People's Republic of China invaded Tibet in 1950, its justification for doing so was to "liberate" Tibet from the control of the British Empire, something that resonated deeply and favorably at the UN, and something that has vexed Tibetans to this day. (Tibetans can't be post-colonial, by the way, because they are currently still colonized.) In a sad way, the situation in Tibet is a result of both a misperceived vision of history and a bit of UN-sponsored racism. The UN could believe that an advanced civilization like Britain had an empire, but when the Tibetans asked for independence from China—well, how could a backward and non-European country like China have an empire? The idea seemed absurd, so Tibet was left in China and the issue was ignored. (And for what it's worth, Tibet also aspired to have its own empire at one point in its history, and so to all the pudding-brained Californians who think that Tibetans are people who spent the entirety of their history meditating, growing organic produce, and weaving yoga mats out of hemp—think again.)

In a previous chapter I discussed the idea of being indigenous and showed how problematic it was in discussions of diversity. I am sure that discussion upset some, but in the current discussion on history and empire and identity, I can show from a slightly different angle why the idea of "being indigenous" creates more problems than it solves. When the UN created the post of Special Rapporteur on Indigenous Peoples, one of the first things the Special Rapporteur was asked to do was to define the word "indigenous." This turns out to be harder than you might think, for both historical and political reasons. José Martinez Cobo, the first person to hold the Special Rapporteur post, offered a tentative definition in a report issued in 1986, and that definition is to a considerable extent still in use today. It defines a society as indigenous if it has "a historical continuity with pre-invasion and pre-colonial societies that developed on their territories."[41] The problem with this definition is that it nowhere defines the word "colonial" or "invasion," and quite predictably, from 1986 to the present the vast majority of countries at the UN have insisted that both of those terms can only apply to white Western countries, since only those countries can be imperialists and colonizers. The result is that there are a rather large number of populations in the world that consider themselves indigenous but are not recognized as such by their governments simply because the majority population in that country isn't white. Those peoples will only be able to obtain justice when the world is ready to admit to all of its imperialism. Just as with the convenient definition of racism in the context of American diversity that automatically denies the possibility of non-white racism, even though it clearly exists, the definition of imperialism as something only white Western people do, though it denies rights and justice to millions of people around the world, is simply too convenient for too many cultures and countries because it allows them to deflect attention from their own historical crimes and blame everything on "the West."

Earlier, for example, I mentioned that the government of China does not recognize the indigenous people of Taiwan as indigenous,

---

41 Jose Martinez Cobo (Special Rapporteur), *Study of the Problem of Discrimination against Indigenous Populations*, UN Document E/CN.4/Sub.2/1986/7Add.4, Pgh 379 (1986)

calling them instead "high mountain people." There is a very specific reason for that—to call them indigenous would imply that China could be a colonial power, but since the Han Chinese aren't white, this is considered impossible, so therefore indigenous people cannot exist. The situation isn't unique to China either—recall my earlier discussion of *La Raza* in Mexico or *mestizaje* in Chile, both of which imply that as one unified population, all are equally indigenous, which is a way of denying any substantive meaning to the idea of indigenousness. To recognize the indigenous people of Mexico as entirely separate would be to imply that the people of La Raza could be colonizers and imperialists, which again, as with China, is considered impossible because La Raza isn't white. The global result has been a considerable *weakening* of indigenous rights, all due to the erroneous interpretation of history that the whole world was as it should be until the white man came. It's an idea as damaging to indigenous rights as it is to diversity itself.

Nostalgia, narcissism, and imperialism
In March 2016, a restaurant and bakery called Saffron Colonial opened in Portland, Oregon, offering a menu that promised a variety of dishes and sweet treats from the days of the British Empire—colonial cuisine, as it were.[42] After complaints from fellow Portlanders, who wanted to keep Portland weird but not *that* weird, a month after opening they changed their name to the British Overseas Restaurant Corporation. A few months later and in another part of the world, in Brisbane, Australia to be specific, the British Colonial Co. restaurant opened its doors, offering not just colonial-themed cuisine but a "stylishly colonial" décor in which to enjoy it. The owners seemed to be taken aback when the

---

42 Rachel Vorona Cote, "Quaint Little 'British Colonial Cuisine' Restaurant Opens in Portland," *Jezebel* (March 20, 2016) at https://jezebel.com/quaint-little-british-colonial-cuisine-restaurant-opens-1766082309

idea sparked outrage among Brisbaners and other Australians.[43] Even more recently, the owner of a privately-run beach club named Punta Canna, located at Chioggia, just a hop and a skip away from Venice, Italy, decided it would be "cute" to offer a bit of Italian nostalgia by using Mussolini-era fascism and imperialism motifs as a decorative theme.[44] The owner was unapologetic after the story came to light, arguing that fascism had provided a kind of order and leadership in Italy that democracy had never been able to offer, and also igniting a debate among Italy's political parties as to whether to shut down the establishment or to tolerate it as an example of democratic freedom of expression.

It would be easy to look at each of these examples as three more pieces of disturbing evidence in the ongoing case of Why White People Don't Get It. Admittedly, there is nothing to defend in each of these examples, and the weird nostalgia that people often develop for times they never experienced has never made sense to me. There are lots of people who love to attend festivals that replicate and romanticize the medieval era in Europe, for example, but those people still want clean, modern bathrooms on site, and would no doubt frown on someone introducing bubonic plague and smallpox into the crowd to create a more authentic experience. But my argument all along in this series has been that it isn't just white people who don't get it—it's everybody not getting

---

43 Elle Hunt, "Outrage at restaurant's homage to 'stylish days' of British empire," *The Guardian* (September 19, 2016) at https://www.theguardian.com/world/2016/sep/19/outrage-at-restaurants-homage-to-stylish-days-of-british-empire

44 Paolo Berizzi, "La spiaggia fascista di Chioggia: "Qui, a casa mia, vige il regime"," *La Repubblica* (July 9, 2017) at http://www.repubblica.it/cronaca/2017/07/09/news/la_spiaggia_fascista_di_chioggia_qui_a_casa_mia_vige_il_regime_-170332052/

it. That, in essence, is the extravagant failure of diversity: it is fueled by the narcissism for ourselves and not, as it should be, by the understanding of others. Part of that lack of understanding reveals itself in misplaced nostalgia, as evidenced in the three examples above. But part of the lack of understanding toward others also reveals itself in the inability to see that the faults and mistakes we attribute to others are also found among ourselves. It's a blindness induced by the narcissism of our current ideas about diversity, ideas that badly and quickly need to be changed.

Self-styled anti-imperialist activists, for example, will work themselves into a rhetorical frenzy over the status of New Caledonia or Hawai'i as colonially-occupied territories, but will remain silent about the status of Taiwan, which is every bit as much a colonially-occupied territory as the others. The same people who claim to see white imperialism everywhere remain blind to all the other imperialisms, the imperialisms of color that have historically been every bit as prevalent as white imperialism. In the case of Taiwan, it is Chinese imperialism that remains hidden from view. China has about as legitimate a claim to Taiwan as Britain does to America, but even the United Nations has developed a vested interest in keeping non-Western imperialisms out of the discussion of global justice, and so the narcissistic blindness of history is replicated even at the international level.

But to bring things back to the United States, let me offer a more specific example of how this peculiar blend of nostalgia, narcissism, and imperialism comes together to undermine the promise and potential of diversity. This example comes in the form of Aztlán, something that emerged as the symbolic focus and rallying cry of the Chicano rights movement in the United States during the civil rights era of the 1960s and early 1970s. Aztlán refers to what many consider to be the ancestral homeland of the Aztec peoples, and for those who endorse the idea behind Aztlán, this territory covers about one-third of the continental United States, stretching from Texas to California. The contemporary embracing of Aztlán as idea and symbol by activist groups in America was that the United States illegally took this homeland away from its people through imperialist acts of occupation and annexation. Aztlán as an ideal thus advocated the retaking of the homeland for its "rightful" owners (including immigration from Mexico to re-populate the homeland) and resisting US imperialism and colonialism.

There are a number of problems with the use of Aztlán as a symbol for a movement advocating equal rights and opposing imperialism, but I want to focus on one specific element just for the purposes of illustration. My point here is to show how the narcissism of identity created by our flawed practices of diversity creates an inability to see the past clearly. In the case of Aztlán, this comes in the form of not seeing Aztlán for what it actually was. Aztlán was less of a homeland and more of a territory, a territory created as part of the Aztec Empire. Yes, that's right, the Aztecs had an empire, and as everyone should know, you can't have an empire without imperialism. Recent archaeological research in Mexico City has uncovered the fabled "tower of skulls" from the former Aztec capital of Tenochtitlan, which was originally thought to have been built from the skulls of fallen warriors under the conquer-or-die approach of the Aztec imperialist elite. What has shocked researchers engaged in this research is the level of violence represented by the tower of skulls—which is about 200 feet in diameter by the way—since one of the unexpected things unearthed in the archaeological dig is that the tower also includes the skulls of women and children.[45] Were these the skulls of sacrificial victims? Did the Aztecs use child soldiers to fight their wars of imperialist conquest? The research is still in progress so we will have to await

---

45 "Aztec tower of human skulls uncovered in Mexico City," *BBC News* (July 2, 2017) at http://www.bbc.com/news/world-latin-america-40473547

answers to these questions, but for now, let's return to the idea of Aztlán.

As a symbolic focus of the Chicano rights movement, Aztlán was meant to invoke two things: (1) the struggle for equality, and (2) the resistance against imperialism. We know with absolute certainty that equality was not a part of Aztec culture or Aztlán society, and as extensive research has made painstakingly clear, Aztec imperialism was every bit as violent and destructive as European imperialism, if not even more so. Yet we still have groups like MEChA (*Movimiento Estudiantil Chicanx de Aztlán*), which are built on the same sort of misplaced nostalgia for the imperialist past as the restaurant examples I mentioned previously. So where does the blindness come from that allows someone to embrace the symbol of one imperialism (Aztlán) and claim it as a symbol of anti-imperialism (against white imperialism)? The answer, once again, is narcissism. Supporters of Aztlán simply cannot see the violence of Aztec imperialism either because they think of it as the process of unifying the people of the homeland (as opposed to the brutal conquest of other societies), or because they think of themselves as the proud beneficiaries of that imperialism (as opposed to being the oppressed victims of European imperialism). Yet, to return to the three examples I started this discussion with, if we are going to filter our interpretations of imperialism as "good" or "bad" based on whether we were victims or beneficiaries, then what's wrong with a white person creating a restaurant in Australia that celebrates the days of the British Empire?

The answer, of course, is that there is everything wrong with it, but—and here's the kicker—there is everything wrong, in exactly the same way, in celebrating Aztlán as well. The examples I gave earlier don't show white people "not getting it," but rather, they show white people doing what every other identity group seems to do—not getting others because they are too busy considering only themselves. Chicano activists make the same narcissistic mistakes as the white restaurant owners, and for the same reasons. We should rightfully denounce imperialist nostalgia, but we need to denounce *all* forms of imperialist nostalgia, including Aztlán, and not just the European ("white") variety. If we push diversity towards the plan I have been advocating all along, where we focus on understanding others rather than on celebrating ourselves, we won't end up with these contradictions, and our narcissism will give way to empathy. That and that alone would be something worthy of the name *anti-imperialist*.

Why making diversity ugly will make it beautiful
I want to return for a moment to the discussion with which I opened this book, of the movie *Eyes Without a Face*, a movie in which the obsession to restore a woman's disfigured face back to a perfect and unblemished visage leads to even more horrifying consequences. Not only is the facial restoration an impossible and futile dream, but also the cost of pursuing the dream—including the murder of other young and innocent women to steal their beauty—is so unacceptably high and so antithetical to the original intent that everything is compromised beyond repair. Confusion and disgust set in, and only when it is too late does the young woman realize that her disfigurement is the face she is destined to have; acceptance becomes its own form of beauty. It is a sobering lesson for those advocates and architects of diversity who continuously strive to create only unblemished beauty for their own particular identity group—beauty of history, beauty of culture, beauty of social life, beauty of everything. The narcissism and self-infatuation that these attitudes induce end up creating a diversity that looks like a newsstand full of men's and women's fashion magazines: nothing but wall-to-wall images of male and female models staring from the covers, each offering an image of perfection and beauty that leaves many an observer feeling imperfect and disfigured.

What most people forget in looking at those images is that the models who smile back from the covers of so many magazines are completely artificial: hundreds and sometimes thousands of photos are taken to find the one that looks perfect, and behind that, an army of make-up experts, lighting technicians, Photoshop professionals, and a whole other entourage of people who spend a good deal of their working days wondering how they ended up in such a vapid profession and why in spite of knowing that they can't seem to walk away from it. They also forget that the images that end up on magazine covers represent a standard of beauty that is as artificial as it is unattainable and undesirable. No one looks like a model in any society except a model. The truly beautiful people will never show up on the cover of a magazine. I've had the chance to speak with acid attack victims in Cambodia, women whose faces were cruelly melted away to the point of losing any trace of their former appearance, women who can't think of lipstick because their lips are gone, and yet their courage, conviction, and kind-heartedness gives me inspiration enough to get me through all of my worst days and to make my best days even better. All this is my way of saying that we cannot build a workable, usable, and viable diversity if we keep trying to make everything beautiful and perfect, if we keep thinking that every culture should be like a model on the cover of Diversity magazine.

When it comes to that other thing, the thing whose evil we cannot comprehend and whose name we cannot speak but will anyway because it is extremely useful to do so—namely (European) imperialism—I could also think of other analogies for why diversity has gone so far off course. Every time I hear someone bring up the topic of imperialism in a discussion of history and identity, I am reminded of the Two-Minute Hate in George Orwell's novel *Nineteen Eighty-Four*. The Two-Minute Hate was a daily routine required of all citizens in which images of the enemies of the regime were projected for the public to see and the public in return was required to vent their anger and hostility against those enemies. The real purpose of the exercise, of course, was to redirect that anger away from questioning the regime itself and to displace it onto something or someone else. If we substitute images of white imperialism, then most discussions of diversity end up becoming something like a continuous loop of the Two-Minute Hate, the real purpose of which is to prevent us from questioning other parts of history that have been equally violent, equally destructive, equally distortive, equally hostile, equally discriminatory, equally despicable, but came from other moments of history when white Westerners weren't even involved. It is as empty a ritual for diversity as it was for civil life in Orwell's nightmarish counter-utopia.

Without a complete revision of history, we end up with so much misplaced anger and so much wasted energy. There were many things that came together to make the morning of September 11, 2001 one of the worst moments in living memory, especially for Americans, but one of those things was the hatred that existed in the mind of one Mohammed Atta for what "the West" had done to his precious little utopia of the past, a utopia he wanted to somehow remake in the present. Whatever hatred Atta felt in his heart was based on a complete misreading of history, a complete misunderstanding of how things came to be, and yet a misreading and a misunderstanding that is not that far off the mark from what currently feeds our visions of what diversity is and what it is supposed to do. If there is anything that gives me a sense of comfort when I reflect on that awful morning in September 2001, it is the fact that, for all of his dreams of a non-diverse utopia where everyone followed the same religion and culture and nothing ever changed, as Atta sits in the hell where he most assuredly is, he is no doubt surrounded by the most diverse group of people in and from history. So much evil has been done by so many people from so many different cultures that hell must surely be a diverse and overpopulated place indeed. So many people are there, from so many different places and different religions and different moments of history, in fact, that hell is going to have be a mighty big structure to contain them all. In my mind, I really hope it's a skyscraper.

INDEX

A
Achebe, Chinua, 74
Aleppo
    and urban history, 114-116
Al-Qaeda, 110-111
animals
    and history, 134-135
Argentina, 26
Atta, Mohamed
    and hatred of diversity, 109
Australia
    early colonization of, 133-135
Aztec imperialism, 165-167
Aztlán
    as nostalgia, 165

B
Boston Tea Party
    as terrorist act, 15-16
Britain
    as post-colonial, 147-148

C
Cambodia
    genocide and authenticity, 116-117
    genocide and identity, 55-56
Chile
    and mestizaje, 27-28
China
    as imperialist, 125-127
chronological narcissism, 114
chronological relativism, 103-104
Columbus, Christopher, 33
CSCOPE, 15
cultural appropriation, 99, 106

D
dependency theory, 87
diversity
    liberal vs. conservative, 64
diversity education
    and re-segregation, 75, 95

divide and conquer
  as imperialist tactic, 156
DWM
  (Dead White Men), 5, 68-70

E
East Side Sushi (2014), 105-106
Egypt, Ancient, 122-124
Eurocentrism
  as non-unique, 75-76
  diversity as antidote, 92
Eyes Without a Face, 1, 56, 168

F
Finland
  as post-colonial, 151
Foucault, Michel
  and history of diversity, 67-68
Frank, Andre Gunder, 83-88

G
Great Wall, China
  as Not-So-Great, 125-126

H
hidden transcripts
  of racism, 49
history textbook controversy
  in Japan, 8-9
hyphen-of-convenience, 37

I
imperialism
  and rise of human species, 131-133
  diversity of, 123-125
India
  non-British empires within, 157-158
indigenous
  UN definition of, 162
Indonesia, 21-22
infanticide
  indigenous, 4
Islamic State
  and reversal of history, 113

L
La Raza, 28-29, 32, 163
Lucy
  as ancestor, 130-131

M
Mahalo Rewards Card, 97
Mayans
  discrimination against, 19
Mericans
  myth of, 30
Mexico
  southern border, 24-25
Morrison, Toni, 80
Mumbai
  name-change and identity, 153-154

N
New Caledonia, 160

nostalgia
    and identity, 163-167

O
Orwell, George
    and Two-Minute Hate, 169-170

P
people of color
    theory of, 53
post-colonial
    as identity, 138
post-colonialism
    as infantalizing, 141

R
racism
    history of, 34
    research on, 46-48
radical history
    and diversity, 77, 82
    as reactionary, 59, 71, 88
Rwanda
    genocide and post-colonial theory, 142-144

S
Said, Edward
    Orientalism and diversity, 71-73
Sima Qian, 85

South Korea
    and racism, 42-46
    nationalist history in, 12
Sri Lanka, 13

T
Taiwan
    and Chinese imperialism, 127-128, 162
Thailand
    and ethnic Chinese, 40
Tibet, 19
    and decolonization, 127, 161
Turkey, 13

U
United Nations
    and incomplete decolonization, 160-161
United States
    as post-colonial, 147

W
walls
    as bad ideas, 26, 130
White Studies
    and diversity education, 79-82

Z
Zapatistas, 31-33

ABOUT THE AUTHOR

D. C. Zook is a writer, musician, and filmmaker who also happens to be a professor at the University of California, Berkeley, in the departments of Global Studies and Political Science. He writes both fiction and nonfiction, and cultivates both sense and nonsense. He is currently at work on two books, one on new frontiers of human rights and the other on the changing landscape of cybersecurity. He is also plotting his next novel, and plotting many other things as well.

Visit D. C. Zook at dczook.com

www.ingramcontent.com/pod-product-compliance
Lightning Source LLC
Chambersburg PA
CBHW051549020426
42333CB00016B/2165